Fishing
THE New River
Valley

M. W. Smith

University of Virginia

CHARLOTTESVILLE AND

University of Virginia Press

© 2002 by the Rector and Visitors of the University of Virginia

Printed in the United States of America on acid-free paper

First published 2002

9 8 7 6 5 4 3 2

LIBRARY OF CONGRESS CATALOGING-IN-PUBLICATION DATA

Smith, M. W. (Michael W.), 1963–

Fishing the New River Valley : an angler's guide / M.W. Smith.

  p.   cm.

ISBN 0-8139-2098-1 (pbk. : alk. paper)

  1. Fishing—New River Valley (N.C.–W. Va.)   2. Fishing—Virginia.

I. Title.

SH464.N53 S65 2002

799.1'1'097557—dc21

2001006530

All photographs by Dwight Dyke,
used courtesy of the photographer
Map by Chris Harrison
ISBN 13: 978-0-8139-2098-6

FISHING THE NEW RIVER VALLEY

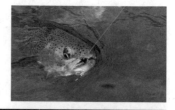

AN ANGLER'S GUIDE

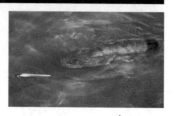

*Dedicated to my grandfathers, who were the first to teach me
the love of fishing, and to Gus, who was always ready to go.*

I care not, I, to fish in seas,

Fresh rivers best my mind to please;

Whose sweet calm course I contemplate

And seek in life to imitate.

—IZAAK WALTON, 1653

Contents

Preface

Welcome to *Fishing the New River Valley: An Angler's Guide.*
Whether you are new to the area or a longtime resident, novice
fisher or pro, this book will provide you with the information you
need to enjoy the natural beauty of the area's waters and to catch
more fish from them. It is my goal to share with the reader the
essential knowledge that I've gained as the proprietor of Greasy
Creek Outfitters (see the appendix) with over 25 years of experience
fishing the New River Valley.

I begin, in chapter 1, by discussing fish species common to the
New River Valley. Chapter 2 covers many of the stocked trout
streams in the New River Valley as listed by county in the
Freshwater Fishing Guide published annually by the Virginia
Department of Game and Inland Fisheries. Here I offer suggestions
on where to fish during the winter months using various cold-
weather techniques and live-bait approaches for trout. I also cover
spinning in the spring, summer, and fall, and fly-fishing on special-
regulation waters.

Chapter 3 concerns itself with fishing Claytor Lake for striped bass and walleye in the cold-weather months and springtime, and smallmouth bass during the spring, summer, and fall. Useful information on catching and using live shad, as well as tackle and lure considerations, can be found here. I also cover two important tributaries of the New River, Big Reed Island Creek and Little River, that enter at the top and bottom of Claytor, respectively.

Chapter 4 offers detailed information on a number of great float trips down the New River, with descriptions of entry and exit points and tips on negotiating the many sets of challenging rapids that the New presents. The upper river (above Claytor Lake) offers excellent walleye and smallmouth fishing, while below the dam muskie, smallmouth, and largemouth are in abundance. I also cover wading at McCoy and Buck Rapids and fishing from boats at Whitethorne and Foster Falls landings.

You'll find in addition a comprehensive map of New River Valley streams, notes on specific fishing locations keyed to maps in DeLorme's *Virginia Atlas and Gazetteer*, and an appendix that lists local guide services, tackle shops, rod and reel repairs, boat dealers, and other sources of assistance and information. This book will tell you where, when, why, and how you will catch more fish in the New River Valley.

When float-fishing streams, safety must be your foremost concern. Local canoe liveries (see the appendix) can provide you with advice concerning river condition and water hazards that may require portage, as well as necessary equipment and floatation devices.

The following is the list of normal stream classifications for rating rapids that are used in trip descriptions throughout this book. If the temperature is below 50°F, or the trip extends through wilderness areas, the river should be considered one class more difficult than normal.

CLASS I: Slow-moving water with small waves and few obstructions. Easy rescue.

CLASS II: Moderate rapids with waves less than three feet high and wide channels that are obvious without scouting. Some maneuvering required. Rescue level of difficulty fairly low.

CLASS III: Formidable rapids with high, irregular waves, often capable of swamping a canoe. Narrow passages that require complex maneuvering and scouting. Rescue difficulty fairly high.

CLASS IV: Long, difficult rapids with constricted passages that often require precise maneuvering in very turbulent waters. Waves are capable of swamping an open canoe. Scouting from shore a necessity, and conditions make rescue difficult.

CLASS V: Dangerous and violent rapids with highly congested routes that should always be scouted from shore. Not for open canoes. Rescue conditions hazardous, with significant danger to life.

CLASS VI: Difficulties of Class V carried to the extreme of navigability. Rescue nearly impossible. For teams of experts only.

Acknowledgments

I wish to thank my wife, Beth, for her editorial assistance and days spent together on the river; Steve Cahill, for sharing his fly-tying expertise; and Mike Keith, who has taught me plenty about fishing the region.

FISHING THE NEW RIVER VALLEY

Fish Species Common to the New River Valley

Largemouth Bass

(Commonly called black bass.) Citation size in Virginia is 8 pounds or 22 inches. The largemouth is dark greenish in color on top with a white belly. A series of black splotches extends laterally along its sides forming a horizontal line to its tail. It has a large mouth and an upper jaw that extends beyond the eye. The dorsal fin is deeply notched. Fish up to 8 pounds are common. Largemouth are found in local ponds, lakes, and streams. Look for them to inhabit the coves and creek mouths in Claytor Lake as well as the edges of the river channel where submerged vegetation, stumps, and logs are located. You can also find them in the main lake near docks and boathouses. They are opportunistic feeders that will eat other fish, crayfish, snakes, frogs, and terrestrial insects. Spawning usually takes place from late April to early June. The best artificial lures include plastic worms, jigs, crankbaits, jerkbaits, spinnerbaits, and topwater varieties.

Rock Bass

(Also known as "redeye.") Citation size in Virginia is 1 pound or 12 inches. This fish is a member of the Sunfish family and rarely weighs more than a pound. It has a short, stout body and a large mouth. Its back is green and its sides can be somewhat golden colored; each scale has a central black spot. Dark spots on its lower body form small stripes. This species is commonly caught by smallmouth anglers on the New River below Claytor Lake who recognize its tendency to provide a ferocious strike with little fight to follow. Rock bass can be found in almost any flowing stream with rocks and ledges. It will eat just about any form of small aquatic and terrestrial life, including crayfish, minnows, and insects, and usually spawns during the same period as the black bass. The best artificial lures include jigs and spinners.

Smallmouth Bass

(Also called bronzeback or "smallie.") Citation size in Virginia is 5 pounds or 20 inches. You can identify smallmouth by its coppery brown color and greenish sides with dark vertical bars. Three dark bars radiate from the cheek across the gill cover. The upper jaw does not extend as far back as a largemouth's, and the smallmouth does not generally grow larger than 5 pounds. The state record came from the New River and weighed 8 pounds 1 ounce. In fact, Claytor Lake and the New River combine for more smallmouth citations than any other body of water in the state. "Smallies" prefer cool, clear water and bedrock ledges, which is why these bodies of water are ideal habitat. Crayfish, madtoms, hellgrammites, minnows, and aquatic insects comprise most of their diet. Spawning normally takes place from late April to early June. The best artificial lures include jigs, spinners, jerkbaits, and topwater varieties.

Spotted Bass

(Also called Kentucky bass.) Citation size in Virginia is not recognized. This fish is similar to both smallmouth and largemouth bass. Its distinctive features include a blotchy lateral band from head to tail and the black spots on its belly. Although it looks a lot like a largemouth, its jaw is not as long, and it usually grows no bigger than a pound. The state record is 3 pounds 10 ounces from Claytor Lake. It is native to the New River and can be found in abundance at the top of Claytor Lake. Kentucky spotted bass feed mainly on insects, crayfish, and small fish. They spawn in the spring at the upper end of the lake. The best artificial lures are similar to those used for large and smallmouth bass.

Striped Bass (and Hybrid Bass)

(Other common monikers include striper and rockfish.) Citation size in Virginia is 20 pounds or 37 inches. This member of the bass

Striped bass, Monorne saxatilis

family has a long body with an olive back, silver sides with solid black stripes extending to the tail, and a white belly. Schools in the 6- to 12-pound range are common on Claytor Lake, while fish in the 30-pound range are a possibility. Stripers migrate up the New in the spring and can be caught at the upper end of the lake and up into the New River as far as Foster Falls. Gizzard shad make up a large part of their diet, and they can often be found close by large schools of shad. Hybrid stripers, introduced to Claytor about a decade ago, share many of the same characteristics. There is a four fish combined limit per day for these fish on Claytor Lake with a 20-inch minimum size. The best artificial lures include bucktails, spoons, big surface plugs, and diving plugs.

White Bass

Citation size in Virginia is 2.5 pounds or 18 inches. This cousin of the striper is native to Virginia. It has a green back that blends into silver sides with whitish bellies, with several broken horizontal lines on its sides and a front dorsal fin that is separated from the rear dorsal. White bass normally reach 2 pounds, while 3 pounds is a citation. They can be caught in the spring months below the Claytor Dam in the New River and at the upper end of Claytor Lake near Allisonia during the annual spawning run. These fish are easy to spot as they chase schools of bait fish to the surface in a feeding frenzy. The best artificial lures include jigs, bucktails, and various topwater minnow/shad imitations.

Channel Catfish

(Also referred to as a spotted cat.) Citation size in Virginia is 12 pounds or 30 inches. Channel cats have a deeply forked tail and a dark silver-gray body that is spotted. It is generally a nocturnal feeder that wanders the bottom of the rivers and lakes for a variety of food sources including crustaceans, fish, and carrion. It can be found throughout the streams and lakes of the New River Valley around rocky ledges and in deeper pools. It spawns in early summer and can be caught using typical catfish baits near the upper end of Claytor Lake. The best artificial lures include anything from jigs to crankbaits.

Muskie

This fish is the largest member of pike family. Citation size in Virginia is 15 pounds or 40 inches. It is usually golden-olive on its back and gray on the sides, with faint spots or blotches running horizontally in a striped pattern. It grows quite large, feeding off of other fish, small animals, and waterfowl. Muskie prefer clear lakes with plenty of vegetation. The state record is a 45-pound fish taken in the New River, which attracts the state's best muskie fishermen. It is not native to Virginia, and populations are maintained throughout the New River mainly through stocking. The best artificial lures include big-game plugs—both topwater and diving varieties—as well as large-bladed spinner baits.

Brook Trout

(Commonly known as "brookie" or mountain trout.) Citation size in Virginia is 2 pounds or 16 inches. This fish species is native to the Blue Ridge Mountains. Its coloring is a spectacular blend of fluorescent purples, yellow, and red spots with faint blue rings around them. The belly is white with distinct red-orange pectoral fins that have a black and a white stripe running vertically on them. A 12-inch native is considered a bragging-rights fish by Virginia standards. The state record brook trout, at 5 pounds 10 ounces, was caught in Big Stony. These trout need clear, cold, cascading creeks with plenty of water flow and small pools. They spawn in the fall and feed mainly on aquatic insects, their larvae, and various terrestrials. The best artificial lures include dry and wet flies, nymphs, and small in-line spinners.

Brown Trout

Citation size in Virginia is 5 pounds or 25 inches. These trout were originally introduced from Europe. Colors vary between olive to golden brown with red and brown spots on the sides. Large males often have a prominent hook jaw feature and colorful orange belly during the fall spawning period. Insects, minnows, and crayfish comprise their diet. They are able to exist in warmer and slower water than brook trout and have adapted well to the region's streams, establishing a thriving wild population. Browns grow large in bigger streams, nearly 15 pounds in some cases. The best artificial lures include dry and wet flies, streamers, spinners, and jerkbaits.

Rainbow Trout

Citation size in Virginia is 4 pounds or 22 inches. This trout is distinguished by its silver sides, black spots, and long pink stripe. The rainbow can also grow quite large; fish of over 14 pounds have been caught in private ponds. They have been imported from the Rockies and are the mainstay of the stocking program in the area.

Rainbows spawn in the early spring months and like fast-flowing rivers as well as deep lakes. The best artificial lures include dry flies, wet flies, streamers, nymphs, and in-line spinners.

Walleye

Related to the sauger and the largest member of the perch family. Citation size in Virginia is 5 pounds or 25 inches. Walleye are typically olive brown with golden flecked sides. The state record (nearly 16 pounds) was taken from the upper New in 2000. In fact, the last four state records have come from the New River, which is home to a unique strain of walleyes that live longer and grow larger than other walleye in Virginia. These fish lie near the bottom of deeper holes in the river by day and move onto gravel sand bars and shallow ledges to feed at night on baitfish, leeches, and crawfish. Walleye spawn as early as February and can be caught from the upper stretches of the lake near Allisonia all the way upstream to Buck Dam during this period. The best artificial lures include jigs, jerkbaits, and crankbaits.

Rainbow trout

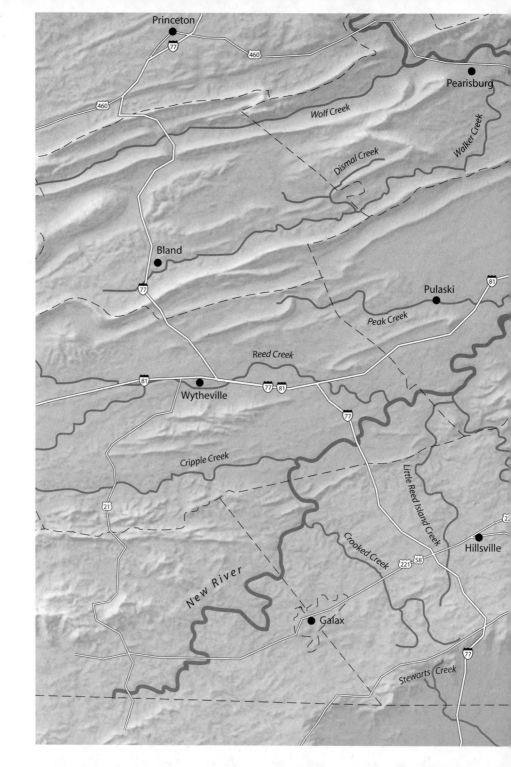

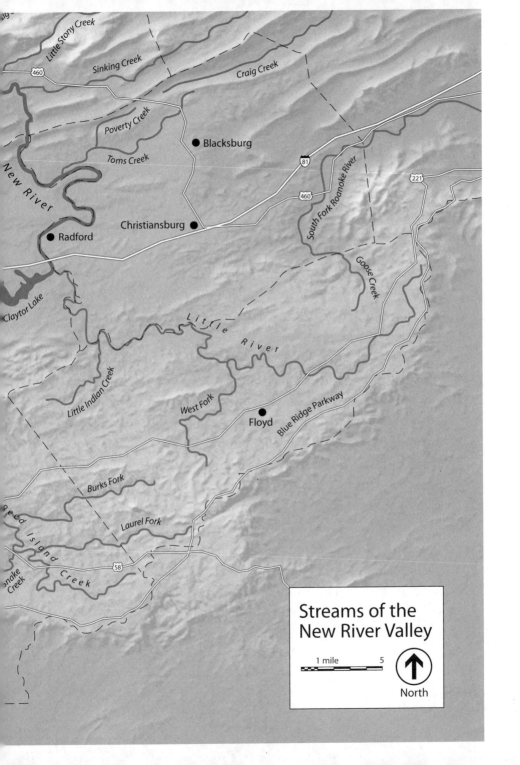

Little Stony Creek

Sinking Creek

460

Craig Creek

Poverty Creek

● Blacksburg

81

Toms Creek

New River

South Fork Roanoke River

221

Christiansburg ●

460

● Radford

Goose Creek

Claytor Lake

Little River

Little Indian Creek

West Fork

● Floyd

Blue Ridge Parkway

Burks Fork

Laurel Fork

eed Island

58

nake Creek

Creek

Streams of the New River Valley

1 mile   5

↑ North

2

Fishing for Trout

Although habitat is declining, Virginia maintains a relatively healthy population of both native and stocked trout species, which include the brook, brown, rainbow, and golden trout. Wild trout populations (of which brook is the only native species) require cool, well-oxygenated water (the familiar cascading pools of the "native" creek) and a clean creek bottom on which to lay eggs. These creeks are often canopied in rhododendron and difficult to access. There are numerous creeks in the Jefferson National Forest that hold native brook trout. The state record brook trout was caught in Big Stony Creek in 1987, but was probably a stocked fish. Many of the native fish are in the 6- to 9-inch range; a 7-inch minimum size limit has been imposed on all trout creeled in Virginia.

Unfortunately, recent studies show that these wild trout streams are in decline due to acid rain and habitat degradation. Poor land-use practices (such as channelization and overgrazing) and unregulated logging methods of the past (now addressed by state and federal laws) have resulted in silting that is detrimental to the feeding and breeding habits of trout. Silted stream bottoms kill trout eggs and decrease the insect life that trout depend on as a food source. Moreover, rising water temperatures caused by decreased stream-side vegetation and loss of fish cover create an unsuitable environment for trout to survive in during the warm summer months. The Department of Game and Inland Fisheries is closely monitoring the over two thousand miles of wild trout streams in Virginia and, these issues notwithstanding, is optimistic about the wild trout resource in the state.

There are approximately 600 miles of stocked trout water in Virginia available for fishing, and over a million fish are stocked annually, according to VDGIF. I remember, as a kid, when anglers would line the banks of the newly stocked creeks in Floyd County on the first Saturday of every April for the opening day of trout season. Thank goodness those days of tangled lines and elbow-to-elbow casts are gone. The state ended its "opening day" in 1996. While it used to be that the winter months were the best time for catching that lunker trout that survived the summer fishing pressure, now that the state has begun a fall-to-spring stocking program, you'll find all sizes of trout abundant throughout the year.

Fall is by far my favorite time to fish, especially for smallmouth and striped bass. But fall is also an excellent time to trout fish, although this season can present some formidable obstacles. The water is usually low and clear, which can make it quite difficult at times not to spook wary trout, and the creeks are often filled with floating leaves that have fallen from the trees. However, fall is also a great time to catch brown trout, which are moving up the small creeks to spawn at that time. If you are lucky enough to have a warm day, a dry fly is a good bet—keep an eye on what's hatching. If not, Prince nymphs are one of my favorite early fall patterns. If you enjoy spinning tackle, try any variety of in-line spinners, such as the Joe's Fly. Another great bait for big brown trout in the fall is a floating Rapala. This lure has produced some big October browns hungry for a hearty meal.

During the winter months, I especially like to fish after there has been snow on the ground for a few weeks and a warming spell brings about a quick thaw. The melting snow has increased the water volume of the creeks, making for better fishing conditions since the fish are more mobile with more water to feed in. In addition, the streams are usually a bit "stained" owing to sediment from this influx of water. (This provides a great opportunity to catch a trophy brown on its favorite food—the night crawler.) Favorable feeding conditions produced by the warm snap will undoubtedly bring the fish out of their usual winter lethargy. I have caught some nice-sized brown trout fly-fishing with gray Hare's Ear nymphs in local creeks during this period.

Early spring fishing offers full streams and, later, the first hatches. During the early months, I stick with old standbys like bead-headed nymphs and Woolly Buggers that go to the bottom. On warm days a March Brown fly pattern can be a good bet. Once the weather begins to warm extensively—end of May, early June—I am ready to fish the river for smallmouth, which are coming off their spawn. By then, trout fishing begins to become difficult, as I find that I have to compete with the snakes, bugs, and vegetation for fishing space in and along most of the creeks of this region. This is a great time, however, to fly-fish the larger streams in the area with duns and dry patterns, such as mayflies and terrestrials. Since stocking ends during the summer months, there are usually fewer fishermen to compete with as well.

Lure selection is always important for trout, especially in determining an effective pattern while fly-fishing. One perennial favorite of many trout fishermen in the smaller creeks of the Blue Ridge where fly-fishing is difficult is the light spinner—Joe's Fly, Rooster Tail, or Mepps varieties. These can be effective baits when live bait isn't an option. I use live bait only when I intend to keep the fish I'm catching, which is only a small fraction of the time I spend trout fishing. (The reason for this is that trout will often engulf a

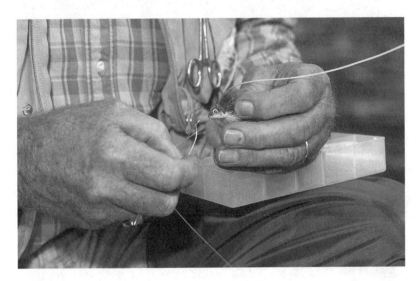

Fly-tying

Stocking trout

night crawler, and the fish will more than likely die if it is hooked internally.)

BIG FISH TIP *Use a 3-inch gold Rapala for big browns in the fall.*

The following streams in and around the New River Valley are traditionally stocked by the Virginia Department of Game and Inland Fisheries. The list is not exhaustive. There are a number of smaller creeks I have not included, such as Goose Creek in my home county of Floyd. Other notable exclusions include Peak Creek in Pulaski County and Toms Creek in Montgomery County. The VDGIF provides a telephone number you can call to check the latest stream stockings by county before you plan a trip: (434) 525-FISH (3474). Stocking information and schedules can also be obtained online at www.dgif.state.va.us/fishing/stock/troutstock.cfm. In the following listings, each watercourse name is accompanied by a reference to the page on which it can be found in the *Virginia Atlas and Gazeteer*, 2d edition (Yarmouth, Maine: DeLorme, 1995).

These are the stocking categories according to the VDGIF trout stocking listing, and are subject to change:

CATEGORY A: Stocked once in each of October, November/December, and January/February; and twice in March, April, and May.

CATEGORY B: Stocked once in November/December, January/February, and March; and twice between April 1 and May 15.

CATEGORY C: Stocked once in November/December, March, and April.

NSF: Waters do not receive fall and early winter stockings.

Carroll County*

Big Reed Island Creek (near town of Laurel Fork)

VIRGINIA ATLAS AND GAZETTEER: 25

DIRECTIONS: From I-77, take Hillsville exit east on U.S. 58 until you reach the creek.

The upper reaches of Big Reed Island Creek have long been known to locals for its holdover wild brown trout and native brook trout populations. Although the creek is no longer stocked, a number of its tributaries are—including Snake Creek, Laurel Fork, and Burks Fork (see below). You can enter the creek under the overpass on U.S. 58 and fish up or down for about a mile until you encounter any houses. I have caught nice-sized browns in this area in the spring. The creek is wide, and occasional pond-sized holes can be found that almost always hold trout until they are caught out over the summer months. There is good fishing to be had anywhere that you can access the creek above U.S. 58 all the way up to The Olde Mill Golf Course; however, this is mostly private property and permission will need to be obtained. The biggest drawback of this stretch of water is that it is occasionally littered with golf balls that make their way down from the headwaters—where the course is located—of this otherwise gorgeous trout reserve.

BIG FISH TIP *Explore—there are numerous bridges above U.S. 58 where the creek might be accessed.*

*Crooked Creek and Snake Creek are covered under the Special Regulations section below.

Laurel Fork (near town of Laurel Fork)

VIRGINIA ATLAS AND GAZETTEER: 25

DIRECTIONS: From I-77, take the Hillsville exit east on U.S. 58. Turn left on VA 654 and follow until you reach the creek. Trout stocking signs will be visible from there.

The stretch of Laurel Fork that is presently stocked is off of Fisherman's Lane. It is clearly marked as such. As a Category A stream, it is stocked from October through May. There is some good water to be found here, but some of the better water on this creek lies downstream at Rainbow Bend (end of VA 661). This area was heavily stocked when I was an adolescent in the mid-1970s, but stocking ceased after some of the land along the creek in that area was bought and subsequently posted. The secret to finding big fish on this stream is to explore. Its headwaters, near Long Mountain, hold some nice native brook trout beneath the canopies of rhododendron. The lower stream, where it widens to nearly 75 feet before entering Big Reed Island Creek, holds some nice wild browns. I have consistently had luck with dry flies in Light Cahill and "mosquito" patterns on summer evenings on Laurel Fork. For spinning fishermen, try a Joe's Fly–Royal Wulff.

BIG FISH TIP *My favorite stretch is from Rainbow Bend to the confluence of Laurel Fork and Big Reed Island Creek.*

Floyd County

Burks Fork (near Buffalo Mountain and town of Willis)

VIRGINIA ATLAS AND GAZETTEER: 25

DIRECTIONS: Take I-81 to VA 8 near Christiansburg. Go south about 22 miles to the town of Floyd. Turn right at light onto U.S. 221. Go approximately 11 miles to the town of Willis. Turn left on VA 764, which will eventually turn into VA 630. Follow until you cross the creek and locate trout stocking signs.

Burks Fork is one of the most popular trout streams in Floyd County. One of two Category A trout streams in the county (the other being Little River), it receives regular stockings every month from October through May. Most of the 5 miles of stocked water

Rainbow trout creel

can be readily accessed from the dirt road that runs along it (VA 630) until its intersection with VA 758 (Buffalo Mountain Road). Browns, "brookies," and rainbows can be taken from its waters on any variety of lures or baits. It is not uncommon to catch the trifecta on an outing to this creek. While much of Burks Fork runs through open pasture, other stretches run up against the steep mountainside leading up to Buffalo Mountain, providing ample habitat for both wild and stocked trout. I have had wonderful success fishing Joe's Flies on ultralight spinning outfits on this creek.

BIG FISH TIP *There are a few places both up and downstream from the stocking area that will offer some great holdover trout fishing for the more adventurous angler.*

Little Indian Creek (Indian Valley)

VIRGINIA ATLAS AND GAZETTEER: 25

DIRECTIONS: From I-81 take the Radford/Tyler Road (VA 177) exit south (same as the new hospital exit). Proceed south on VA 600 to Childress and turn right on VA 693. After a few miles, turn left at the intersection of VA 787 (Indian Valley Road). This is a winding road that you will follow alongside Little River for approximately 5 miles until you reach the bridge that crosses over it into Floyd County. Continue up VA 787 until you begin to see Indian Creek and the trout stocking signs on your left. You will cross it numerous times as you continue toward its headwaters. The creek is stocked in the spring (Category B) the entire way until you cross it for a final time and it disappears to your right.

With its many clear plunge pools and long runs, Indian Creek was once a fantastic native fishery. It was nearly spoiled when a Roanoke newspaper ran an article about the creek and it was subsequently fished out, as it is so easily accessible from top to bottom by Indian Valley Road. Only a few years ago, it was common to catch a limit of native brook trout in its headwaters on almost every trip. This is still a spectacular put-and-take creek, offering easy fishing in a robust atmosphere of tall standing pines, big boulders, and occasional rock overhangs.

BIG FISH TIP *Try Big Indian from the confluence with Little Indian up to VA 631.*

Little River (near the town of Floyd)
VIRGINIA ATLAS AND GAZETTEER: 25

DIRECTIONS: Take I-81 to VA 8 near Christiansburg. Go south on VA 8 about 18 miles to VA 705. Turn left and follow about 1 mile until you cross Little River and locate trout stocking signs on VA 706.

Little River is a large trout stream for this region. It is over 100 feet across in some stretches where stocking takes place. If it were not for the warming of this shallow river in the summer and the silting due to the many farms that line its banks upstream, this trout fishery might be tremendous. As is, much of this Category A stream is fished out before summer by the numerous bait fishermen who line up to fish the deeper holes, and the fish that are left head upstream in search of the many cool, gravel-bottomed feeder creeks that supply the Little River with its mediocre flow. I have fished nearly the entire length of this river from where it begins in the upper reaches of Floyd County near the Blue Ridge Parkway (for wild browns), to the area called Bear Cub Falls near the Montgomery County border (for smallmouth bass). Much of the land along its banks is private farmland, and thus the river is accessible only by canoe. This is one option that you can explore for fishing this river and catching holdover trout that have made their way upstream or have been washed down as far as Sower's Mill Dam.

The stretch of the river that is regularly stocked (mostly with rainbows) runs along VA 706 in both directions for about 3 miles and can be easily accessed throughout.

BIG FISH TIP *Try a float trip in the spring.*

West Fork Little River (near town of Willis)
VIRGINIA ATLAS AND GAZETTEER: 25

DIRECTIONS: Take I-81 to VA 8 near Christiansburg. Go south on VA 8 about 22 miles to the town of Floyd. Turn right at light onto U.S. 221. Go approximately 7 miles to VA 729. Turn right and follow the road until you see trout stocking signs on the left.

I recently fished this fine freestone creek in the middle of the summer, after an extended period of rain had muddied up the New River too much to fish on for a couple of weeks. I was pleasantly surprised to find a number of holdover rainbow trout ready and willing to take my fly. I fished most of the day with an Adams pattern and caught four nice rainbows, and there wasn't another fisherman in sight. I have been told by a fly-fishing friend that he lost count of his catch on one wading trip through the cornfields upstream. West Fork runs through acres of pasture, and thus is a relatively low-gradient stream, with some deeper holes and undercut banks that hold a hearty population of regularly stocked trout. This is a Category B stream and does not receive fall and early winter stocking.

BIG FISH TIP *Fish above U.S. 221 to the confluence of Rush Fork, which is also stocked.*

Fly-fishing

Giles County*

Big Stony Creek (Jefferson National Forest—White Rocks Recreation Area)

VIRGINIA ATLAS AND GAZETTEER: 41

DIRECTIONS: Take U.S. 460 from Blacksburg west past Pembroke until you see the signs for White Rocks Recreation Area. Turn right on VA 635 (Big Stony Road). This road will take you to the stocked portion of the stream and all the way up to White Rocks (approximately 17 miles from U.S. 460).

Big Stony is a popular Category A stream, receiving regular October to May stockings. There is approximately 6 miles of stocked water to fish along this easily accessed creek. The "bigger" water downstream is often fished hard by the live-bait fishermen with much success. Further upstream, near where the Appalachian Trail crosses the creek, you'll find classic Blue Ridge trout water in abundance. There are lots of overhanging rhododendrons, quiet pools, and the large stones that give the creek its name. Spinning fishermen may want to try Joe's Flies, while fly-fishermen might find a Muddler Minnow or Adams Fly successful. When the water is up in the springtime, try nymphs on the lower portion of the creek for bigger fish that have washed down during stocking.

BIG FISH TIP *There are several good native feeder creeks in the area worth trying. But please practice catch-and-release on these fragile streams.*

* Little Stony Creek is covered under the Special Regulations section below.

Dismal Creek (Jefferson National Forest—Dismal Falls)
VIRGINIA ATLAS AND GAZETTEER: 40
DIRECTIONS: Head west from Blacksburg on U.S. 460. Turn left on
VA 730, just before crossing Sinking Creek. Follow this road until
you reach VA 100 at Staffordsville. Turn left and go about 2 miles to
VA 42 at Poplar Hill. Turn right and follow until you reach VA 606,
then turn right again and go north until you reach Dismal Falls
parking lot.

   The drive out to Dismal Creek is worth the trip, if only to see the
wonderful falls themselves. There is fishing at the falls, but the terrain is difficult. I would suggest going further upstream to either
Walnut Flats or White Pine Horse, which allow public camping.
Dismal Creek is a Category B stream that does not receive fall and
early winter stocking.

BIG FISH TIP *Explore the other creeks in the area such as Nobusiness and Wolf.*

Montgomery County

Craig Creek (Jefferson National Forest—Brush Mountain)
VIRGINIA ATLAS AND GAZETTEER: 41
DIRECTIONS: From Blacksburg, take U.S. 460 west to VA 621. Turn
right and follow about 5 miles to the Caldwell Fields area. Trout
stocking signs are posted throughout.

   I have found this Category B stream difficult at times to fish for a
number of reasons. It is extremely shallow and clear, and does not
receive heavy stocking. You will often find fish only in the deeper

pools where they are stocked, ones that are not likely to dry up in the summer, since this creek has been prone to low water levels recently. Still, it is a fun creek for those who don't mind a tedious presentation and smaller fish. For fly-fishermen, I suggest using 5x or smaller tippet and a Number 18 Black Ant or terrestrials. Since this creek is in the National Forest, close to Blacksburg, it sees heavy fishing pressure by put-and-take fishermen.

BIG FISH TIP *Explore the National Forest dirt roads along VA 621.*

Poverty Creek (Jefferson National Forest—Pandapas Pond Recreation Area)

VIRGINIA ATLAS AND GAZETTEER: 41

DIRECTIONS: Take U.S. 460 west from Blacksburg to VA 708/FR 269. Turn left and follow until you see the trout stocking signs.

I like to park at the last point where the creek turns south away from the dirt road and hike downstream as far as possible. This area gets quite remote, and the freestone creek offers a series of deep green plunge pools and long runs that are home to hefty holdover rainbow trout. Like Craig Creek, its sister creek across U.S. 460, Poverty Creek receives heavy put-and-take pressure. This is designated a Category C stream that receives one fall, one winter, and one spring stocking.

BIG FISH TIP *Pandapas Pond is also stocked.*

South Fork Roanoke River

VIRGINIA ATLAS AND GAZETTEER: 41

DIRECTIONS: From I-81 at the Christiansburg exit, take U.S. 460 south to Shawsville. Turn right onto VA 637. Proceed up this road until you see trout stocking signs on the left.

The section of this river that is in Montgomery county is relatively shallow and small, consisting of a number of feeder branches that begin in Floyd County as "native" creeks (such as Purgatory and Goose) and end up passing through the cities of Salem and Roanoke as part of the Roanoke River. The lower portion of the creek that is stocked is rather flat and wide enough to easily fly-fish. Small spinners can also be very effective for lure fishermen. I like to fish as far upstream as possible, where the gradient is higher and

Spin-cast fishing, south fork Roanoke River, Montgomery County

the pools holding fish more pronounced. This is a Category A stream that receives regular stocking from October through May. As of January 1, 2001, the section of the Roanoke River above Salem at Green Hill Park (1 mile upstream of VA 760) receives a delayed-harvest program offering excellent catch-and-release trout fishing.

BIG FISH TIP *Some big browns have been caught in the city of Salem.*

Special Regulation Waters

Restrictions have been placed on certain wild trout waters as well as several types of stocked trout streams. The following list covers the best stretches of these creeks and offers some tips on fishing them.

Crooked Creek (Carroll County, 5 miles east of Galax)

VIRGINIA ATLAS AND GAZETTEER: 24

DIRECTIONS: From I-77 south, exit at Hillsville. Drive west on U.S. 221 about 3 miles until you see a sign for the Crooked Creek Wildlife Management Area. Turn left on VA 620 and go about 3 miles until the road becomes a dirt lane leading into the facility.

This is primarily a fee-fishing area that is open from 7:00 A.M. to 6:00 P.M. from April to September. A daily permit costing $4 is required and can be obtained at the fee-fishing facilities on the right as you drive in. The area consists of approximately 7 miles of stocked trout-fishing water, where you can catch brook, browns, and rainbows. In addition, an upper section to this stream is regularly stocked by the Virginia Department of Game and Inland Fisheries as a Category A stream and is well worth the fifteen-minute drive from the main fishing area. I have done quite well there on bead-headed nymphs and streamers in the early spring. From late spring to early summer, you can consistently take fish throughout the stream on standard match-the-hatch patterns. The pristine, tumbling streambeds offer some outstanding fly- and spinning tackle fishing, and have yielded numerous citations over the years.

BIG FISH TIP *Explore the East Fork.*

Little Stony Creek (Jefferson National Forest, at the Cascades)
VIRGINIA ATLAS AND GAZETTEER: 41

DIRECTIONS: From Blacksburg, take U.S. 460 west to Pembroke where a Jefferson National Forest sign indicates the Cascades. Turn right here onto VA 623 and follow 4 miles to the parking area.

Near the town of Pembroke, the Cascades area is heavily used by hikers and can be reached easily from U.S. 460 via VA 623. Special regulations (single hook, artificial lure only, 9-inch minimum size) apply to the portion of the creek that lies below the Cascades waterfall. This stream is not stocked and relies on a healthy wild population to renew itself naturally. The upper reaches of Little Stony contain native brook trout, while the lower section contains both brook and rainbow. Get an early start when fishing Little Stony, as there is plenty of water to fish here. Almost every one of the deep, blue-green pools that you will encounter holds a trout or two. I have had some success here on a Royal Wulff pattern in the past, but caddis and mayfly imitations are a sure bet if the hatch is on. Expect to catch your limit and then some on a trip to this wonderful mountain stream, but you won't want to keep any of these beautiful wild fish. This is a good trip to bring a nonfishing companion who likes to hike and enjoy the scenery. Expect to share the trail with hikers going to the waterfall.

BIG FISH TIP *There's good "native" fishing above the Cascades.*

Chestnut Creek (Carroll County—Delayed Harvest designation)
VIRGINIA ATLAS AND GAZETTEER: 24
DIRECTIONS: From I-77 south, take the Hillsville exit onto U.S. 58 west, then turn right onto VA 887 at the public boat landing sign. Follow about 2 miles to Wolf Glade and turn right onto VA 635. Continue about 3 miles to Hebron and turn left onto VA 736, then

Fly-fishing—rainbow trout

turn left onto VA 793 at Riverhill. After about 2 miles you will reach the creek. Parking is available across the bridge on the right at the New River Trail State Park access. The trailhead in Galax at U.S. 58 provides another large parking area approximately 11 miles upstream of the first access described. A third access lies at the bridge on VA 607; you can reach it by turning left off of VA 635 at Hebron.

I have been fly-fishing Chestnut Creek on a regular basis since it received Delayed Harvest status in 2001. This is a stream that really benefits from its designation as a special regulations fishery, allowing trout to locate throughout the stream and holdover across the entire 11 miles of stocked water between the town of Galax and the creek's confluence with the New River. The New River Trail, which parallels Chestnut Creek, allows access to these more remote regions and yields wonderful surprises and great rewards. Rock ledges, boulders, and large pools characterize the lower reaches of the stream, which also produce big smallmouths in the springtime, while the upper half of the creek is trout heaven, replete with riffles and runs. Every spring, my wife, daughter, and I enjoy hiking the trail and nymphing the occasional pool, in which small stocked rainbow trout are always plentiful and holdover surprises abound.

BIG FISH TIP *Try your luck at Chestnut Falls, upstream of the VA 607 access.*

Snake Creek (Carroll County, near Fancy Gap)
VIRGINIA ATLAS AND GAZETTEER: 25
DIRECTIONS: From I-77, turn east at Hillsville onto U.S. 58. Turn right onto VA 674 at Red Hill. Then turn left on VA 922.

Special regulations apply (single hook, artificial lure only, creel size of 12 inches) to all of Big Snake Creek below Hall Ford and all of Little Snake Creek below the junction of VA 922 and VA 674. Snake Creek is a moderate-gradient, gravel-bottomed stream with an average width of 18 feet. Native brook trout are also present. While this creek has allowed bragging rights to some local trout fishermen in the past, recent low water levels have led to a decline in the harvest of large-sized fish. I last fished the Snake on a Saturday afternoon in mid-November, shortly after a period of rain. The creek was up, but running clear, and I had less success than I had expected upon arrival. Still, undisturbed by any other fisherman, I found that this beautiful area, with its pristine setting, made the trip worthwhile.

BIG FISH TIP *Try the section between the confluence of Big and Little Snake down to the U.S. 58 bridge (which is a good access point).*

Stewarts Creek (Carroll County, near Lambsburg)

VIRGINIA ATLAS AND GAZETTEER: 24

DIRECTIONS: Follow I-77 south past the Blue Ridge Parkway to the Lambsburg exit, VA 620. Go through Lambsburg and turn left onto VA 696, then turn right onto VA 795, which ends at the Stewarts Creek Wildlife Management Area.

Besides the Roanoke River, this is the only stream included in this book that is not part of the New River watershed. Stewarts Creek actually drains into the Yadkin River in North Carolina. Special regulations apply (single hook, artificial lure only, catch-

and-release). The best fishing starts about a mile upstream of the parking area (there is a path) where the South and North Forks meet. The South Fork is the larger of the two and leads vertically up the mountainside toward Sam's Knob. There are good numbers of sizable brook trout thriving in the many plunge pools and water-falls found on this creek.

BIG FISH TIP *Practice stealth.*

3

Fishing Claytor Lake

Consisting of nearly 5000 acres of water, Claytor Lake was
impounded on the New River in 1939 by the Appalachian Power
Company. The lake spans over 20 miles of the Pulaski County
countryside, south of I-81. According to the Virginia Department of
Game and Inland Fisheries, over the years the lake has been stocked
with species of fish ranging from walleye to striped bass to gizzard
shad. Largemouth, smallmouth, spotted, white, and hybrid striped
bass can all be taken from its waters. The three black bass species
listed above (the first three) are regulated by a 12-inch minimum
size and a limit of five per day (all three species combined). Striped
bass are stocked annually in the lake, and some have been caught
that weighed over 30 pounds. The hybrid species was introduced in
1992 and is doing quite well. Harvest of these two species combined
is four fish per day (20-inch minimum size). Claytor Lake provides
the best white bass spring run anywhere in the state, and it far sur-
passes all state waters in annual citations in this category. Kentucky
spotted and smallmouth bass are native to its waters and can be

found in abundance throughout the lake. Good crappie, bluegill, and catfish action (both flathead and channel) can be had as well.

Boat Landings on Claytor Lake

Allisonia Public Landing (on VA 693)

VIRGINIA ATLAS AND GAZETTEER: 24

DIRECTIONS: From I-81 take the Hillsville/VA 100 exit south. Drive until you cross the New River bridge. Turn left onto VA 608 at Barren Springs. Follow until you cross Big Reed Island Creek and the road ends at VA 693. Turn left and follow the VDGIF public boat landing signs until you reach the lake.

The public landing at Allisonia is often crowded on February and March nights with fishermen in coveralls who will spend the cold night trolling for walleye. One old-timer told me of past nights when the fish were so thick that fishers could literally gig them. While the walleye are running, most people troll the area between the rapids in the river that mark the upper end of the lake and the old Norfolk and Western train trestle at Hiwassee a mile or so downstream. Just below it lies a good set of ledges running horizontally across the lake. The most effective technique is to position your boat upstream and slowly work back and forth across the river from shore to shore. Be careful of the lines from the many fishermen dotting the bank when the run is on, especially up near the rapids. I suggest using Storm, Yozuri, or Countdown Rapalas in the 3-inch range; chartreuse or orange colors are often effective.

As the winter walleye run begins to wane, the striper and white bass hybrid begin their spring trek up river to spawn; so it is common in April to find boats drifting downriver and casting bucktails to the bank, then trolling back upstream hoping for either species of fish. I like to use 7-inch broken-back Rebels up near the rapids at night for these fighters. Also, heavier tackle, such as 20-pound test, can make the difference in landing these fish or losing them. I have caught some nice hybrids on topwater shad imitations (such as the Spit'n Image or Zara Spook) during the spring in these waters.

Below the old Norfolk and Western Railroad bridge (now donated to the New River Trail by Norfolk Southern), the river begins to widen into the lake and there is some deep water that is worth fishing for catfish and striper, especially with live shad if you can find them. Try throwing a cast net up in the rapids or any of the nearby coves. Any size up to 12 inches is good striper bait. Put a sinker about 2 feet above the bait and let it swim on the bottom. Keep your bail open because striped bass hit on the run. Many rods have left the boat unannounced while fishing live gizzard shad for stripers!

Another good place to fish for stripers is right across from the Allisonia boat launch. I have caught numerous 15-pound fish in this area and seen a few in the 25-pound class taken from this water in the spring months! The technique I use here, where the river channel is less than 10 feet deep, is to tie on a swivel with about a 6-foot leader and a large hook. (The size of the hook will depend on the size baits that you are using. Too large a hook will kill the fish and hamper its mobility.) Tie a balloon above the swivel and float downstream with the baits out 20 to 30 yards behind. You may have to use a trolling motor to keep the boat from turning and tangling your lines.

During the summer months, I like to fish this area of the lake for smallmouth bass, especially with topwater baits. The lake is fairly shallow at this end and there are numerous underwater ledges that make it almost like fishing the river. My favorite lures include such shad imitations as Spit'n Image, Zara Spook, and Big Dog-X. Sometimes it takes numerous casts to find fish that are willing to feed on top, but when you do the rewards can be enormous. Usually these lures produce fish in the 2- to 4-pound range, and the strike is tremendous.

BIG FISH TIP *Walk the dog—i.e., use shad imitation, topwater lures to work the many underwater ledges that cross the river.*

Claytor Lake State Park and Hidden Hollow public boat landings (I-81 at Dublin to VA 660)

VIRGINIA ATLAS AND GAZETTEER: 41

DIRECTIONS: Take I-81 south to VA 660/State Park Road. Go south until you see the signs for the first boat launch at Hidden Hollow on the right, or continue straight to the concrete landing at Claytor Lake State Park. Camping and other facilities are available. For information on Claytor Lake State Park call (540) 674-5492.

Due to the deep cool trough in the riverbed created by Claytor Dam, there is excellent bass fishing at this end of the lake, but I tend to fish this area mainly for striper. A good way to start is by trying topwater plugs at night around the islands. I like to troll fluorescent orange broken-back Rebels very slowly through this area within sight of the dam during the summer nights. Winter fishing can also be quite productive at this end of the lake. Cold, crisp December nights will yield striper to the angler willing to bear the elements. Fish big Rebels, Red Fins, and Shad Raps by casting the banks on a slow retrieve. For smallmouth, try using deer-hair jigs on schooling fish in late winter and early spring.

Many fishermen resort to jigging spoons in the winter months. This is an effective way to catch bass, walleye, and perch. Another option for any time of the year is to bring a cast net and catch shad for live bait rigging. (Try the back of Dublin Hollow). This consists of placing a ½- to 1-ounce barrel weight and a bead above a swivel, then a leader tied to the swivel with a large hook. The size of the

Claytor Lake State Park, Pulaski County

hook will depend on how big the shad are that you are using. Then troll the baits beneath the boat with the weight slightly above the bottom. This is how many of the bigger fish on the lake are caught. If you prefer to fish for largemouth, there are numerous hollows on the south side of the lake that offer some good fishing as well. Plastic worms, jig-and-pigs, and plastic jerkbaits such as flukes are very productive in this area.

BIG FISH TIP *Slow-troll big shallow running plugs at night near the islands.*

Harry DeHaven Park (VA 663 / Poor House Road)

VIRGINIA ATLAS AND GAZETTEER: 41

DIRECTIONS: Get off I-81 south at the Radford/VA 232 exit just before the New River bridge. Turn at the VDGIF sign onto VA 605/Little River Dam Road. Follow VA 605 about 6 miles to VA 663/Poor House Road. Turn right and follow the VDGIF signs to the boat launch.

This new public landing at Harry's Point has good ramps and public facilities, including a fishing pier that is handicapped accessible. I arrived at this launch about five o'clock one morning and was greeted by a school of feeding striper that had run bait up into the cove. I quickly tied on a big topwater plug and caught some nice fish right there off the bank!

This landing is convenient for fishermen and boaters who live on the south side of the lake, as it allows them access to its bottom half. (The only other launch on this side is up at Allisonia.) From here, you can easily shoot down to the dam and fish the Dublin Hollow area or go up the lake to some of the better coves and creeks that line its southern shore, including Clapboard Hollow (which can also be a good place to catch shad). Then fish the channel across the lake on its northern shore between there and Lighthouse Bridge. I have caught some nice striped bass in this area during the fall and spring of the year. Also, try deer-hair jigs for pre-spawn smallies holding on mid-depth structure in the spring.

BIG FISH TIP *Fish the structure in the main part of the lake, especially points, before heading into the coves.*

Peak Creek, Rock House Marina, and Lighthouse Bridge (off I-81 and VA 100)

VIRGINIA ATLAS AND GAZETTEER: 40–41

DIRECTIONS: From I-81 south, take the VA 100 exit south at Dublin and you will pass Rock House Marina on your left after a few miles. There are launches here and at Conrad Brothers Marina. Continue across Peak Creek to VA 672 and turn left. You will come to Lighthouse Bridge in about 2 miles. The landing is on the right before you cross the bridge.

These are all private launches with a fee. You can fish anywhere within Peak Creek and out to the lake for a variety of species of fish. These include smallmouth and largemouth bass, white bass, striper, and crappie. Peak Creek holds a good population of large-mouth bass. In fact, the VDGIF reports that a 14-pound, 6-ounce monster was taken from this area in 1991. The best way to catch white bass is to find the schools with a fish finder and use live minnows. For smallmouth, try using deer-hair jigs on schooling fish in late winter and early spring.

For striper, I like to catch bait up in the creek, near the I-81 bridge, and then troll my way out toward the lake with live shad on a bottom rig. I troll as slowly as possible, keeping the bail open with light resistance on the free spool setting. When a striper hits it will run hard and fast; merely cranking on the reel with a sharp upward pull will usually set the hook and start the drag to stripping. It will take some time to troll out to the mouth of Peak Creek, but there is good fishing in that area of the lake. If you go out and up the lake around the Lighthouse Bridge (or put in there) in late fall, watch for striper to break in the late afternoon and cast 1-ounce bucktails to the open water. A fish finder will help, as this area of the lake is deep.

BIG FISH TIP *Try from the Lighthouse Bridge down to Clapboard Hollow for striper in November and throughout Peak Creek in April.*

Two Key Tributaries

There are two vital tributaries of the New River just above and below Claytor Lake that are well worth fishing in their own right: Big Reed Island Creek and Little River. The latter begins in Floyd County and reaches the New River just below Claytor Dam. Avid canoeists in the area are probably more familiar with the former—a medium-gradient creek flowing through primitive Carroll County. There are three trips on Big Reed north of U.S. 221 to its confluence with New River near the upper end of Claytor Lake, and two trips on the Little River north of VA 8 to the Little River Dam at the bottom of the lake.

Big Reed (U.S. 221 to VA 753)

DISTANCE: 5 miles

VIRGINIA ATLAS AND GAZETTEER: 25

DIRECTIONS: (1) *Put-in.* From Hillsville (off I-77) take U.S. 221 north toward Floyd about 5 miles until you cross the Big Reed Island Creek Bridge. Turn right after crossing and park. (2) *Take-out.* From U.S. 221 at the put-in, go north past the hamlet of Dugspur and turn left on VA 764, then follow for about 2 miles until you reach the intersection of VA 753. Turn left and go approximately 4 miles until you reach the bridge that crosses Big Reed Island Creek. Parking is visible on the left.

This is a fun float with its share of small Class I rapids and long, slow runs that hold fish. It can easily be made in a half a day, and there is good access at both the put-in and take-out. Dean Rogers and I have had great success in the fall using live crayfish in some of the deep holes—but soft plastics and Rapalas can also provide some good action. I am partial toward spinners and jerkbaits in the spring and topwater plugs in the summer. There are two very deep, elongated holes marked by car-sized boulders on this float—one near the beginning and one near the end. Be sure to stop at these if you have brought along any live bait.

BIG FISH TIP *Use live bait in the fall for big smallies.*

Big Reed (VA 753 to VA 764)

DISTANCE: 8 Miles

VIRGINIA ATLAS AND GAZETTEER: 25

DIRECTIONS: (1) *Put-in.* From U.S. 221 at Hillsville (off I-77), go north past the town of Dugspur (about 8 miles) and turn left on VA 764, then follow for about 2 miles until you reach the intersection of VA 753. Turn left and go approximately 4 miles until you reach the bridge that crosses Big Reed. Parking is visible on the left. (2) *Take-out.* From I-81 take the Hillsville/VA 100 exit south. Drive until you cross the New River bridge. Turn left onto VA 608 at Barren Springs. Follow the VDGIF public boat landing signs until you reach VA 693, then turn right and follow for about 3 miles to the two-lane bridge that crosses Big Reed. Turn left onto VA 764 just before the bridge. This is a dirt road that you will follow for approximately 4 miles until you pass Big Falls. You can take out anywhere river access is available up to the confluence with Greasy Creek near VA 765. *Note:* The best route for shuttling between the take-out and put-in is to continue on VA 764 to the intersection with VA 611 and turn right. Follow until it ends (about 2 miles) and turn right onto VA 753, which will bring you to the put-in.

This is a pleasant all-day float through remote country with scenic rock outcroppings and limestone creek bottom. One interesting feature is the tunnel on the left near the end of the float that was blasted by loggers years ago, allowing some of the creek to flow though the mountainside and back into Big Reed about 5 miles downstream, below what's called Big Falls. The take-out for the

float is just above these Class III rapids, which are a favorite swim-
ming hole for locals. The fishing is good throughout this stretch,
with fish under 12 inches plentiful. The bigger fish are often wary
and easily spooked in the clear, quiet pools.

BIG FISH TIP *Stop above the many holes and wade them with either live bait
or lures.*

Big Reed–Claytor Lake (VA 764 just above VA 693 bridge to Allisonia Public Boat Landing)

DISTANCE: 6 miles

VIRGINIA ATLAS AND GAZETTEER: 24

DIRECTIONS: (1) *Put-in.* From I-81 take the Hillsville / VA 100 exit
south. Drive until you cross the New River bridge. Turn left onto
VA 608 at Barren Springs. Follow the VDGIF public boat landing
signs until you reach VA 693, then turn right and go about 3 miles
until you meet Big Reed at the two-lane VA 693 bridge. Turn left
onto a dirt road (VA 764) before crossing the creek, and find
parking along the creek. (2) *Take-out.* From I-81 take the Hills-
ville/VA 100 exit south. Drive until you cross the New River bridge.
Turn left onto VA 608 at Barren Springs. Follow the VDGIF public
boat landing signs until you reach VA 693, then turn left and go
about 2 miles to the lake.

There is some great fishing on this, the final stretch of Big Reed
Island Creek, and its confluence with the New River at the upper
end of Claytor Lake. Although the creek runs alongside the road for
a good portion of this float, and in fact crosses under two bridges,

don't be surprised by the quantity and quality of the fish you will catch. I have done quite well with topwater plugs, such as Pop R's and Torpedoes, in the fall by casting across underwater ledges and drop-offs. I like to use soft plastics here in the summer. Live bait can also be productive—one spring I caught a hefty channel catfish in one of the deep holes on this float using a live creek chub. An acquaintance who lives on the creek has caught numerous 3- to 4-pound fish over the years through here.

BIG FISH TIP *Try plastic flukes.*

Little River (Montgomery–Floyd County line, VA 8 to VA 787)

DISTANCE: 15 miles

VIRGINIA ATLAS AND GAZETTEER: 41 and 25

DIRECTIONS: (1) *Put-in.* Take I-81 to VA 8 near Christiansburg. Go south on VA 8 about 10 miles to the bridge that crosses Little River. Turn right just before it, and go under the bridge to find parking and canoe access. (2) *Take-out.* From I-81 take the Radford/Tyler Road (VA 177) exit south (same as the new hospital exit). Proceed south on VA 600 to Childress and turn right on VA 693. After a few miles, turn left at intersection of VA 787 (Indian Valley Road). This is a winding road that you will follow alongside Little River for approximately 5 miles until you reach the bridge that crosses over it into Floyd County, with a number of access points visible along the way. *Note:* The best route for shuttling from the take-out to the put-in is to continue on VA 787 across the Little River about 1 mile and turn left on VA 740. Follow approximately 5 miles to VA 750 and turn left. This road will end at VA 8. Turn left and you will soon cross the Little River at the put-in. CAUTION: This is a two-day float that is extremely difficult, harboring many hazards. Others have lost their lives at Bear Cub Falls.

While there are numerous floats that can be done on the Little River in Floyd, I prefer one notorious stretch known as Bear Cub Falls. Like many before me, I did not know what I was getting into the first time that I made this float. It can hardly be made in a day if you want to do the extraordinary fishing any justice—even during the long days of midsummer. My fishing partner and I realized this as we finally finished the arduous Bear Cub Falls portage around dusk, only to find that there was still nearly 4 river miles of paddling yet to come. Fortunately, the river is rather serene beyond the falls, presenting only a few Class I rapids to contend with, and we had the foresight to bring a flashlight just in case. The moral of the story is that this is a difficult float, best done with an experienced guide.

Lower Bear Cub Falls themselves are formidable Class IV+ rapids that form a mini-gorge at the entrance. This must be portaged to the right. You will know that you are approaching the gorge proper as you begin to see large boulders lining the river and hear the noise of whitewater. Get out here and scout. There is a path about a half mile in length in the woods that will take you around the gorge. Preceding the gorge is a wicked, narrow bend on river right with a 3- to 4-foot drop-off that must be carefully portaged as well. I once witnessed some friends roll a canoe and lose some supplies here—a scary sight in the turbulent water. This dangerous stretch of the river follows a steep-gradient, nearly mile-long series of drop-offs, shallow ledges, and mini-islands that present a painstaking and time-consuming task to traverse. I call this area the "power-line shoals," and you will know that you are nearing them as you cross under massive power lines and the river widens considerably. Plan on at least an hour to cross the shoals and an hour portage at the gorge, exclusive of time spent fishing.

A number of sand bars line the river just above the shoals and between Upper Bear Cub Falls and the Lower Bear Cub Falls, making ideal places to camp. I usually like to float two-thirds of the way on the first day to the upper set of falls, which are a single Class III–IV falls that should be portaged on the left. I have rolled a canoe by trying to make it through this fall on the right. Just below the upper falls, you will find a long deep stretch of water and a number of smaller rapids that make for good fishing, especially with live bait. I like to make camp in this area and wade it in the evening and the next morning before embarking on to the shoals and eventually the Lower Bear Cub Falls on the second day.

The first part of this float—from the put-in to the upper falls (approximately 10 miles)—offers some fantastic small-stream fishing through rolling rapids and long slow pools. I suggest stopping above these pools and taking turns with your partner wading and tossing plugs into these areas. Fly-fishing can offer great rewards as well, if you are willing to make the effort. There is one area in particular that I like to fly-fish on this float, near Camp Carysbrook—a high-gradient, elongated set of ledges and rapids with a number of small, divergent falls and plunge pools, each holding its share of feisty smallmouth. This is a difficult area through which to navigate the canoe, but a lot of fun to fish if you have the time. You'll reach it about 4 miles into the trip. (Do not confuse it with Upper Bear Cub, which is approximately 6 or 7 miles further.) This is one of several stretches of this float that are slow going owing to shallow-water ledges and broad shoals over which the canoe will have to be walked or lifted and carried.

There is excellent fishing throughout this entire float. The terrain is largely remote, and you will see only a few farmhouses or cabins and even fewer people. I can recall a two-day trip on which we caught a dozen smallmouth over 16 inches—the largest fish was nearly 20 inches and easily weighed over 4 pounds.

BIG FISH TIP *I suggest big topwater plugs such as the Chug Bug, Pop-R, or Torpedo, and soft plastic worms.*

Little River (Montgomery–Floyd County line on VA 787 to Graysontown Bridge on VA 693 to Little River Dam on VA 605)
DISTANCE: 2.5 miles to Graysontown. 10 miles from put-in to the Little River Dam.
VIRGINIA ATLAS AND GAZETTEER: 41
DIRECTIONS: (1) *Put-in.* From I-81 take the Radford/Tyler Road (VA 177) exit south (same as the new hospital exit). Proceed south on VA 600 to Childress and turn right on VA 693. After a few miles, turn left at the intersection of VA 787 (Indian Valley Road). This is a winding road that you will follow alongside Little River for approximately 5 miles until you reach the bridge that crosses over it into Floyd County, with numerous access points visible along the way.

(2a) *Take-out at Graysontown.* From I-81 take the Radford/Tyler Road (VA 177) exit south (same as the new hospital exit). Proceed south on VA 600 to Childress and turn right on VA 693. After a few miles, pass the intersection of VA 787 (Indian Valley Road) and proceed about 2 miles to VA 613. Turn left and travel about a mile until you come to the river. You can park at the left side of the Graysontown Bridge and find river access. (2b) *Take-out at Little River Dam.* Get off I-81 at the Radford/VA 232 exit just before the I-81 New River bridge. Turn left at the VDGIF sign onto VA 605. The dam is about 2 miles on the left. You will have to plan ahead for this float, as you must call the City of Radford at (540) 731-3603 and get a parking permit for access to the boat launch. *Note:* The best route for shuttling from the take-out to the put-in is to continue on VA 605 about 2 miles to VA 664. Turn left, cross the Little River, and follow for about 2 miles, then turn right onto VA 787 (Indian Valley Road).

The first section is a relatively short float with a few slow-rolling rapids and a single Class I along the way. I recommend fishing the deeper bank on river left during the first part of the float with lures such as spinners and Rapalas in the spring, and soft plastics and topwater varieties in the summer months. You might want to try live bait, such as hellgrammites, in the rapids and deeper pools that occur later into the float, but be prepared to catch plenty of redeye if live bait is your preferred tactic.

You will reach the take-out point at Graysontown before you know it and will probably want to keep fishing on through

Snowville. However, river access is nearly impossible, as most of the land along VA 693 is now posted. One option is to continue all the way to the Little River Dam. If you choose to make the float to the dam, I would recommend starting at the Graysontown Bridge, as this, in itself, is a 6- to 7-mile float with better than a mile of slow water near the end. As you go through the Snowville area, you will pass under two bridges and encounter a number of houses along the road. There is some excellent fishing in this stretch. In fact, I know of a 5-pound smallmouth that was taken from here in spring 1997. Once you pass under the second bridge (on VA 693) the rest of the float is remote, passing through some serene farmland and wooded hillsides. You will eventually pass the Radford University outpost on the river and then reach the pond above the dam. In its entirety (about 10 miles) this a long, small-river float—be prepared for extensive paddling.

BIG FISH TIP *Try topwater plugs, soft plastic flukes, or live bait.*

4

Fishing the New River

In the New River, James River, Rappahannock River, and the Shenandoah River, Virginia offers some of the finest smallmouth fishing anywhere. Popular belief holds the New to be among the oldest rivers in the world and one of only a few that flow from south to north. From its origin in the higher mountains of North Carolina, near Blowing Rock, it flows northward through the mountains of Virginia some 160 miles into West Virginia.

The New offers a variety of fishing opportunities that range from catfish to muskie to a rare spotted bass. State records for smallmouth, walleye, and muskie have been recorded from its waters since 1987. By far the most abundant, the "bronzeback" is also the most popular fish among anglers. There is a 14- to 20-inch slot limit (no bass within that range) on bass, with a combined limit of five fish (all black bass species combined), in effect on the entire New River through Virginia. In accordance with the Trophy Fish designation of the river, one bass in excess of 20 inches may be kept per day. There is an 11- to 14-inch slot limit (no bass within that range) on bass, with a combined daily limit of five fish (all black bass species combined), in effect below Claytor Lake.

The stretch of the river that traverses the New River Valley proper divides into two obvious sections—above and below Claytor Lake—with distinct differences. The section above is generally more primitive and remote, while the section below flows through the town of Radford and out along U.S. 460 to West Virginia. Each offers the angler different species of fish. Above, you will find walleye, and in the spring months, striped and hybrid bass that have come up from the lake to spawn. Below you will find rock bass (or "redeye"), largemouth, and muskie. Smallmouth and channel catfish are abundant throughout. Since the fish species and their habitats vary, I fish both sections differently as well.

When preparing for a float on the New River I'll often spend the evening before seining a nearby creek for crayfish and throwing a cast net for creek chub and shiners. Although I enjoy plug fishing and using plastic baits on light spinning tackle through much of the river, I sometimes find it irresistible to stop and fish beneath the many sets of rapids that the New offers with a good live bait. These are also good places to seine for hellgrammites. Such methods consistently offer some excellent fishing for big smallmouth. Because these fish will run with the strong current below sets of rapids, you need some backbone to land them. A size 8 hook and a medium split shot on 8- to 12-pound test line and a sturdy live bait rod are all you need to catch fish.

For lure (especially topwater and jerkbait) presentations, I like to fish medium-action spinning rods with open-face ultralight to light spinning reels and 6- to 8-pound test monofilament line. I usually have one reel spooled with a thin-diameter braided line, up to 10-pound test, to use for soft plastic baits and jigs. These new brands of line are much more sensitive than the monofilament, allowing you to feel every twitch. I will carry anywhere from two to four rods, depending on whether or not I am in a canoe or a boat, how many people are with me, and whether or not I need one specifically set up for live bait on a particular trip.

BIG FISH TIP *One of the best baits for New River smallmouth is hellgram-mites.*

The following pages describe various wading opportunities, canoe floats, and boat trips from specific landings, including the newest

Spin-cast fishing on the New River

addition to the State Park Service at Foster Falls off U.S. 52. Organization is by county, following the south-to-north flow of the river through the New River Valley. There are numerous liveries (including one at Foster Falls) and professional outfitters in the area that can prepare you for a float if you need their services (see the appendix). Always wear a life vest while paddling or wading. The New has many sudden drop-offs and undercut ledges, and is prone to sudden changes in water flow due to the many dams that are located on it. *Note:* You can compute travel time for fishing on the following floats at approximately 1 mile per hour.

Grayson County

Baywood (U.S. 58) to Riverside (VA 94)

DISTANCE: 8.5 miles

VIRGINIA ATLAS AND GAZETTEER: 24

DIRECTIONS: (1) *Put-in.* From I-77 south, take the Hillsville exit onto U.S. 58 west/U.S. 221 south toward Galax. About 6 miles past Galax you will reach the New River. The public boat landing sign and exit is on the right off U.S. 58 just before crossing the New. (2) *Take-out.* From I-77, take the Hillsville exit onto U.S. 58 west/U.S. 221 south toward Galax. Just past the town of Galax, take a right onto VA 94. Cross the river and go about 4 miles until you see the public boat landing sign at Riverside.

At just over 8 miles, the Baywood-to-Riverside trip is the perfect length for a day-long summer float. The first portion of the float is rather slow, and there are a number of trailers and home sites along

Canoeing on the river

river left, but the latter portion is as picturesque and pleasant as any. About 2 miles into the trip the terrain becomes more remote and the river takes on an awesome complexion. Boulders line the shoreline and are strewn across the riverbed, producing eddies and pools that are effective places to anchor and fish with a live bait or lure. The final half of this float—especially between Bowyer's Ferry and Joyce's Rapid (Class II)—offers some spectacular smallmouth fishing. I last fished this stretch in the middle of the summer and found that the area around Joyce's Rapids consistently yielded fish in the 16-inch range on Heddon Torpedoes. It would make an excellent place to fly-fish as well. You should negotiate this rapid through the middle, so as to avoid the large rocks on the left side. Near the end of the float you will see VA 94 on the left bank. The take-out is on the left near the intersection of VA 274 and VA 94.

BIG FISH TIP *Move quickly through the upper portion of this float so that you can concentrate on the better water near Joyce's Rapids.*

Riverside (VA 94) **to Oldtown** (VA 641) **to Fries Dam** (VA 94)
DISTANCE: 5.5 miles to Oldtown; 8 miles from Riverside to Fries Dam
VIRGINIA ATLAS AND GAZETTEER: 24
DIRECTIONS: (1) *Put-in.* From I-81 south, take the VA 52 exit south at Fort Chiswell, then turn right onto VA 94. Follow this road approximately 20 miles until you reach the town of Fries. Turn right and follow VA 94 south about 4 miles until you reach the New River; turn right onto VA 274 and you will see the signs for the public boat landing. (2a) *Take-out at Oldtown.* From the town of Fries, follow VA 94 south until you reach the New River (near the Riverside public boat landing). Turn left and continue until you cross the New River bridge. Go about a half mile and turn left onto VA 634, which you will follow about 2 miles until you reach VA 641. Turn left and it will take you to the public boat landing at Oldtown. (2b) *Take-out at Fries.* From I-81 south, take the VA 52 exit south at Fort Chiswell, then turn right onto VA 94. Follow this road approximately 20 miles until you reach the town of Fries. There is an informal take-out just above the dam on VA 94.

I really enjoy the upper stretch of this two-part float right from the start. The gentle rapids and the deep holes they produce just below the boat launch hold nice fish. I remember starting a float here one midsummer morning and hooking into a 3-pound smallie on a Pop-R the very first cast from the canoe! I consider the first couple of miles of this float to be the best water. One could easily wade this area as well. You should concentrate on the ledges and deep water on the southern bank (right side) of the river. A bit further downstream the same shoreline is lined with willow trees that make a good place to fish a plastic worm or topwater bait. There are also a couple of islands and grass beds that can be productive grounds for soft plastic jerkbaits. The river gets shallow around the VA 94 bridge and the fishing is by and large not as good from here on out. One blemish of this stretch becomes evident near the end of the float where you will see literally hundreds of old tires littering the otherwise clear shallow river bottom. The take-out at Oldtown is on the right about 2 miles downstream of the VA 94 bridge.

The second stretch of this two-part float gets mixed reviews as well. It is troublesome to note the effluent that dumps into the river near the Oldtown boat launch: there are some great deep-water ledges on the east bank just below the pipe that one hardly wishes to fish because of the discoloration and the smell. However, once you pass this area the fishing gets very good—the river widens and an elongated series of ledges cross the river. The river is difficult to chart through here when low water produces a rock garden effect, but a healthy flow results in some Class I rapids. There are numerous pools that hold 16-inch and better fish in these rapids. The shoreline in this area is quite productive and yielded a near-citation fish to outdoor writer Bruce Ingram (on a Crippled Killer) during a summer float we made together. The last portion of the trip will require some paddling through the pond above the Fries Dam. The take-out is on river left just above the line of blue barrels that cross the river. This is a poor boat landing that requires you to carry canoes and tackle up a steep hill to a wayside that is over a hundred yards away!

BIG FISH TIP *One word—topwater.*

Carroll County

Fries (Riverside Park, off VA 94) **to Byllesby Pond Public Boat Landing** (VA 739)

DISTANCE: 7 miles

VIRGINIA ATLAS AND GAZETTEER: 24

DIRECTIONS: (1) *Put-in.* From I-81 south, take the VA 52 exit south at Fort Chiswell, then turn right onto VA 94. Go south approximately 20 miles to the town of Fries. You can launch at the VDGIF public boat landing in Riverside Park. (2) *Take-out.* From I-77 south take Hillsville exit onto U.S. 58 west, then turn right onto VA 887 at the public boat landing sign. Follow about 2 miles to Wolf Glade and turn right onto VA 635. Continue about 3 miles to Hebron and turn left onto VA 736 for a short distance until reaching VA 739, then turn right. This road ends at the landing. *Note:* The best route for shuttling from the take-out to the put-in is to backtrack to Hebron and turn right onto VA 607, which you will follow to VA 721. When you reach VA 721, turn right and it will bring you to the bridge that crosses the New River and VA 606 leading to Fries.

This is an exciting float with numerous rapids and ledges. There is great fishing just below the dam for starters. Once you embark down the river, you will cross under a bridge that has an informal launch area on river right (parking here is nearly nonexistent, however). Be especially cautious of the series of Class II–III rapids at Double Shoals soon after. I suggest scouting before attempting to run them, as the water level is constantly changing. After you pass these, the river presents an interesting feature of plentiful boulders that run for about a mile and offer some outstanding fishing. I have caught some nice smallmouth in this area (called the "boulder fields" by locals) as well as largemouth that come up from the Byllesby Pond area. Many fishermen in this area concentrate on big bass by using big topwater baits such as Torpedoes and Crippled Killers.

After passing the "boulder fields," you will soon float under another bridge. Below it, the river begins to slow, becoming placid as you approach the Byllesby Pond. High cliffs and wooded shoreline make the scenery through this area breathtaking in places. After at least a half hour of steady paddling, the boat landing will appear on river right. Be aware that on this float the water level of the river may fluctuate due to release at the Fries Dam.

BIG FISH TIP *Try soft plastics.*

Fowler's Ferry (off VA 635), between Byllesby and Buck Dams
(off VA 94; VA 602 to VA 737)
DISTANCE: N/A
VIRGINIA ATLAS AND GAZETTEER: 24

DIRECTIONS: From I-81 south, take the VA 52 exit south at Fort Chiswell, then turn right onto VA 94. Travel south about 15 miles on VA 94 until you hit VA 602 in the Jefferson National Forest. Turn left onto VA 602. This will take you to the Byllesby Dam (approximately 3.5 miles). When you reach the dam, turn left onto VA 737. You can tube-float or wade any of this area between the two dams, a distance of about two river miles. There is an informal launch on the other side of the river as well, accessible via VA 635.

There is public camping for a nominal fee via the honor payment system (part of the Mount Rogers National Recreation Area off VA 94) near Buck Rapids (Class II–III) that will provide good wading access to the river between the two dams. Mike Keith has taken some big fish in this area while wading with live bait in the many pools it offers. There is exceptional lure fishing here as well. In fact, my biggest smallie of 1998 (a 20-inch citation) came from this stretch of the New and hit on a 4-inch Smithwick Rattling Rogue. Be aware when wading this area that the water level may rise abruptly due to release at the Byllesby Dam, and always wear a floatation vest.

BIG FISH TIP *I highly recommend this area to tube-float fishermen.*

Wythe and Pulaski Counties

Ivanhoe (VA 94) **to Austinville** (VA 69) **to Foster Falls State Park** (off U.S. 52 and VA 608)

DISTANCE: 5 miles to Austinville; 10 miles from Ivanhoe to Foster Falls

VIRGINIA ATLAS AND GAZETTEER: 24

DIRECTIONS: (1) *Put-in.* From I-81 south, take the VA 52 exit south at Fort Chiswell. Then turn right onto VA 94 and continue 9 miles until you reach Ivanhoe. Follow the signs to the New River Trail (left off of VA 94) onto Riverview Road. Continue straight under the trestle on the river road to one of the many informal put-ins that dot the river. Following this road (VA 764) past the gauging station and to the end will bring you out again to VA 94. (2a) *Take-out at Austinville public boat landing.* From put-in, backtrack on VA 94 north to VA 619 east. Turn right and follow VA 619 until you reach the bridge at Austinville (VA 636/VA 69). Turn right and cross. The boat landing is on the left once you cross the river. (2b) *Take-out at Foster Falls.* From I-77, take Exit 24, then turn left onto VA 69 a short distance to U.S. 52 (where state park signs will direct you to the landings). Turn left onto U.S. 52 and go 1 mile to VA 608. Turn right and follow until road ends at park gates. Entry will cost $2. *Note:* The best route for shuttling from the take-out to the put-in(s) is to backtrack to I-77, pass under the Interstate and follow VA 69 all the way to the Austinville public boat landing, which will be on the right before you cross the New River.

This two-section float starts in Wythe County near the Jubilee Park fairgrounds, just below Buck Dam. The river road offers easy access and begins a scenic float that holds many breathtaking cliffs and long stretches of relatively uninhabited riverbank. If you are willing to negotiate some tricky ledges, a trip up the river to the dam can provide some excellent fishing. However, you will need a light boat with a jet motor. If you are content to start fishing at the put-in, the east bank is usually the most productive area at the start of this float, at least until you travel through the first set of Class I rapids and leave behind the campers and makeshift cabins that dot the western shoreline. From that point, focus attention on the rocky western bank.

Early in the float you will pass under an old Norfolk and Western train trestle that is now part of the New River Trail. There are a number of shale ledges below the trestle that provide excellent deep-water fishing and a long run of Class I rapids. There is excellent fishing in this area for both smallmouth and walleye. I registered an 8-pound, 10-ounce citation "eye" through here in August 1996. Further downstream, the two sets of Class I–II rapids above the Austinville boat ramp should be approached with caution. Scout first! The first, with a more difficult drop, can be taken through the middle when water levels are conducive. Otherwise portage to the left. CAUTION: Just downstream of this rapid a line of metal stakes crosses the river diagonally.

A public boat ramp has been opened in Austinville by the VDGIF, which will allow you to cut the length of the float in half; otherwise, you can continue on the second section of the float to Foster Falls. The water is almost still in this area and will require at least half an hour of steady paddling to traverse by canoe. (Another shorter section of still, deep water occurs just after passing under the I-77 bridge above Foster Falls.) Two large sets of Class II rapids occur as you come within sight of the I-77 bridge, and should be negotiated with caution. I recommend taking the first set to the right and the second set to the left. You will find a number of good ledges to work below this last set of rapids. Ray Hart once caught a 24-inch striper coming off its spawning run in these rapids here in early June on a plastic grub.

Through this portion of the river, I normally fish light-to-medium action spinning outfits with 6- to 8-pound test and use surface or shallow running jerkbaits. I have had good luck on 4-inch gold and silver Rapalas, 5-inch broken-back gold and orange and black Cordells, and 3-inch chartreuse Rapala Husky Jerks. I use these lures in this part of the river because they are effective for both walleye and smallmouth, and are relatively easy to work under a variety of conditions—from deep, slower pools and eddies, to fast currents below rapids, to long casts across the shallower shoals. I also keep a rod rigged with some sort of plastic bait— a worm, grub, or fluke. Of course the colors for all baits vary depending on the season, time of day, and the clarity of the water, but my favorites are usually motor oil, salt-and-pepper, and pearl white.

Fishing for walleye

Live bait is also an option below the many sets of rapids. I like to anchor as close as I can safely get and work the baits down with the flow. The best baits are creek chubs, crawfish, and hellgrammites. Heavier tackle is good here. I cannot count the number of times I've gone to set hook on a drifting bait only to have the fish snap the line and just keep going. It's possible for you to run into a 30-inch muskie in this area (as I once did), or a 10-pound catfish (likewise) while bass fishing. Either species can hit a lure or live bait when you least expect it!

This is an excellent float. Many citation walleye and smallmouth have been caught in this stretch of the New River. Furthermore, the state record walleye (15 pounds, 15 ounces) was caught in this area in December 2000. This float ends at Foster Falls, which is itself an excellent area to fish either by canoe or by carefully wading between the upper and lower sets of falls. Near the I-77 bridge you can catch a glimpse of the historic shot tower in which molten lead was dropped to form musket balls during the Civil War. Many people come to this area of the river for these attractive reasons.

BIG FISH TIP *Use jerkbaits, especially in stained water.*

Foster Falls State Park (VA 608, off U.S. 52)

DISTANCE: N/A

VIRGINIA ATLAS AND GAZETTEER: 24

DIRECTIONS: From I-77, take Exit 24 east to U.S. 52, where state park signs will direct you the landings. Turn left and go approximately 1 mile to VA 608. Turn right and follow until road ends at park gates. Entry will cost $2. See below for camping information.

The facilities at Foster Falls are some of the newest of the Virginia State Park family, offering reservation camping, livery, boat launches, and even equestrian trails. Canoes and johnboats can be rented in the park from New River Adventures (see the listing in the appendix). The New River Trail passes through the park as well and affords fishermen the opportunity to wade the long dual set of Class III–IV rapids that create the spectacular falls themselves. Many nice fish have been caught here by wading fishermen using small jigs and light tackle.

The New River Trail State Park, 57 miles long and an average of 80 feet wide, forms a continuous link between Claytor Lake and the town of Fries. The land was donated to the state by Norfolk Southern Railroad in 1986 and is part of the "Rails to Trails" program. It includes two tunnels, three major bridges, and numerous smaller bridges and trestles. Camping is allowed at Millrace and Cliffview campgrounds (reservations required). For more information contact New River Trail State Park at (540) 699-6778.

The Foster Falls park includes two landings, one above and one below the falls. The upper landing will allow you to access a mile stretch of fairly deep water up to and above the I-77 bridge over the river. This is excellent water for walleye and catfish. With a "jet" drive or small johnboat you can fish all the way up to the falls above the bridge, offering some very good smallmouth fishing during the summer. The lower landing will allow you to fish the large hole that forms at the bottom of the falls for walleye and smallmouth, or a rare striper that has come up from the lake on the

spring spawn. This is an excellent place to hunt for a citation walleye in the early spring, as Mike Keith and I found out a few years
ago when we hooked into a couple of 20-inch-plus fish on white
bucktails with fire-pink tails.

BIG FISH TIP *Fish from the lower landing below the falls for walleye in the*
early spring.

Foster Falls (VA 608) to Allisonia (boat ramp off VA 693)

DISTANCE: 13 miles

VIRGINIA ATLAS AND GAZETTEER: 24

DIRECTIONS: (1) *Put-in.* From I-77, take Exit 24 east to U.S. 52, where
state park signs will direct you to the landings. Turn left and go
approximately 1 mile to VA 608. Turn right and follow until road
ends at park gates. Entry will cost $2. (2) *Take-out.* From I-81, take
the Hillsville/VA 100 exit south. Drive until you cross the New River
bridge. Turn left onto VA 608 at Barren Springs. Follow the VDGIF
public boat landing signs until you reach VA 693, then turn left and
go about 2 miles to the lake. *Note:* The best route for shuttling from
the take-out to the put-in is to backtrack on VA 608 to VA 100,
cross, and continue until you reach the Foster Falls park. CAUTION:
this "ribbed" dirt road becomes quite treacherous as it descends
Foster Falls Mountain.

This stretch of the river ranks as my favorite and presents some
unique features, including long ledges that run parallel to the bank
for hundreds of yards at a time. There are also a number of rustic

cabins that sit back beyond the floodplain. (In fact, one of these is the very cabin that I stayed in as a boy when I learned to fish the New.)

You will want to put in at the bottom boat landing, below Foster Falls. Stay to the right of Baker Island and fish the runs below the sets of Class I rapids that you travel through as you go by the island. Once you pass the island, the river becomes tricky. First, there is ledge running across the entire river that creates a 2- to 3-foot set of falls and Class II rapids. Negotiate this on the far right. Soon after this, you will encounter the long ledges that run down the center of the river. These can be quite dangerous. I like to stay to the far right and ride the long chute out to the bottom of this section. There is some good fishing in this area, but it is not worth the headache of trying to find a successful way to fish it.

Once you are below these parallel ledges, you will find a series of good fishing spots for the next couple of miles, each made up of a Class I rapid followed by long deep runs. The fishing through this stretch can be outstanding at times, especially when using Rapalas, jig-and-pigs, and topwaters (Heddon Pop-R's and Torpedoes are my favorites), or live baits in the many pools you will pass through. This is an extremely long float packed with "fishable" water that you will not want to pass up. Both smallmouth and walleye can be had from these waters, and I have seen some 40-pound catfish caught on lay-lines.

Watch for an elongated set of solid Class II rapids (Bertha Shoals) about a third of the way through the float that should be scouted and negotiated on the right. This is an outstanding area, which is well worth taking some time to wade and fish. There are a couple of sets of Class I rapids just above Bertha that will alert you that you are getting close. To the right, you will see some cabins in the distance and may see hikers and bikers on the New River Trail.

Another good landmark to note is the VA 100 bridge which you will pass under about two-thirds of the way through the float. Once you pass the bridge, be prepared to paddle some slow, deep water for about a mile. There is good fishing near the end of this stretch where numerous ledges line the river. There are also a number of Class I rapids to traverse. Be sure to leave time to fish some good water near the end of this float—above and below the mouth of Big Reed Island Creek (on river right). The couple of ledges below the confluence mark the upper end of the lake, and the take-out is shortly after that on the right. This float will take all day, so an early start is a must, especially during the spring or fall when daylight saving time is not in effect.

BIG FISH TIP *Go with topwater plugs.*

City of Radford and Locale

Public Landing below Claytor Dam (off VA 605) **to Peppers Ferry Bridge** (VA 114)

DISTANCE: 10 miles

VIRGINIA ATLAS AND GAZETTEER: 41

DIRECTIONS: (1) *Put-in.* Get off I-81 at the Radford/VA 232 exit just before the I-81 New River bridge. Turn left at the VDGIF sign onto

VA 605. The landing is about 1 mile on the right. (2) *Take-out.* From Blacksburg, take U.S. 460 east to VA 114. Turn right and drive toward Radford. Proceed until you cross the New River at Peppers Ferry Bridge. You will find the launch area under the bridge on your left. *Note:* The best route for shuttling from the take-out to the put-in is to drive through the town of Radford. To do this, continue on VA 114 to Fairlawn. Turn left at the light onto U.S. 11. Cross the New River and turn right onto VA 232. This will take you to VA 605, where you will see the sign indicating a public boat landing. Turn right onto VA 605; the landing is about 1 mile on the right. CAU-TION: Be aware that the river may fluctuate drastically in water level due to the release of water from the dam.

There are numerous ledges along this float and some Class I rapids, both of which are good areas to find bass lurking, especially if there are grass beds or water willow nearby. Be careful at the last set of rapids (Class II) just above the Peppers Ferry Bridge and take-out point. Depending on the level of the river, these can often prove tricky and require some caution. Not long ago, a boy drowned here.

This float can be cut in thirds by finding a number of informal landing sites through the town of Radford, Bisset Park, or near Deadmond Center. Soft plastic jerkbaits, in-line spinners, and top-water plugs provide good action here. Also, tie on a muskie plug to throw before dark. My longtime fishing buddy, Sterling Herbst, has employed this tactic to some success on this float. Just be sure that you have proper tackle and nets to tangle with one of these monsters while fishing out of a canoe.

In the springtime, I like to take my boat and slow-troll the area between Claytor Dam and the I-81 bridge. You will want to position your boat upstream and slowly zigzag across the river horizontally. This can be an effective way to catch various species of bass that have run up the river in an effort to spawn. Also, try the mouth of Little River.

BIG FISH TIP *Try below the dam at night for walleye in October.*

Peppers Ferry Bridge (at VA 114) to Whitethorne (off VA 623)

DISTANCE: 8 miles

VIRGINIA ATLAS AND GAZETTEER: 41

DIRECTIONS: (1) *Put-in.* From Blacksburg, take U.S. 460 east to VA 114 in Christiansburg. Turn right and drive toward Radford. Proceed until you cross the New River at Peppers Ferry Bridge. You will find the launch area under the bridge on your left. (2) *Take-out.* From Blacksburg, take VA 685/Prices Fork Road to VA 652 and turn right. Proceed to Longshop and turn left onto VA 623, at the VDGIF public boat landing sign. Follow until you cross the railroad tracks and find the boat launch. *Note:* The best route for shuttling from the take-out to the put-in is to backtrack on VA 652 to the intersection with VA 659/Prices Fork. Turn right and travel about 3 miles until you reach VA 114 and turn right. From there, follow the directions above to the put-in.

The Peppers Ferry to Whitethorne section cruises through the Radford Arsenal and holds some dangerous Class II–III rapids that lie a mile or so below the put-in. These should be approached on the right side and with extreme care. It is probably best to portage this stretch if possible. Above and below there is excellent fishing, as this stretch of the river doesn't receive too much fishing pressure. There are a number of good bends to fish as you pass through the arsenal, although the river slows some as you near Whitethorne and is often filled with aquatic vegetation in the summer months. For this reason, the Whitethorne Landing seems to attract plenty of muskie fishermen. As you approach Whitethorne there will be an island in the river that is best fished through the right.

There is some excellent smallmouth fishing through the arsenal, especially in the "burning grounds" area—an explosives test site for the Arsenal. Should you hear a warning siren, you must vacate immediately. This is also muskie territory and is a favorite area for muskie fishermen. Don't be surprised to inadvertently hook one while fishing for smallmouth. The state record muskie (45 pounds) was caught on the New in July 1989. They have been known to hit everything from Rebel Crawdads to topwater baits. And a hungry muskie will even strike a hooked smallmouth on the retrieve—as many of us who have fished this area for years can attest to!

BIG FISH TIP *Think muskie.*

Montgomery County

The Whitethorne Landing (off VA 623)
DISTANCE: N/A
VIRGINIA ATLAS AND GAZETTEER: 41

DIRECTIONS: From Blacksburg, take VA 685/Prices Fork Road to VA 652 and turn right. Proceed about 3 miles to Longshop and turn left onto VA 623, at the VDGIF public boat landing sign. Follow until you cross the railroad tracks and find the launch.

This water offers some exceptional fishing over a broad range of fish species. The river is deep near Belspring, where a number of citation muskie and smallmouth have been caught. From there, you can look for largemouth, Kentucky spotted bass, and smallmouth bass in abundance in the deep water that follows. Some very large bass have been taken at night in this area by fishermen trolling black spinner baits.

I don't recommend fishing this stretch of river by canoe for two reasons. One, the slow current near Belspring means an hour of steady paddling down to Parrot. Two, at Parrot, the river forms shallow shoals that entail a continuous effort at "walking" the canoe through to reach the open water above McCoy rapids. This is a much better area to drive out to and wade (see following section). If the river is up and you do decide to make this run, the multitude of shallow ledges at Parrot can be fished effectively with plastic worms and topwater plugs. There is an informal landing at McCoy off VA 625. It's best to fish Whitethorne from a boat, however, and either float down and motor up, or vice-versa. You can go up into the "burning grounds" section of the Arsenal from this landing as well, depending on the size of the boat and the level of the river.

BIG FISH TIP *Try a jig-and-pig in the spring.*

Wading at Parrot and McCoy Rapids or "Big Falls" (McCoy Junction off VA 625)

DISTANCE: N/A

VIRGINIA ATLAS AND GAZETTEER: 41

DIRECTIONS: From Blacksburg, take VA 685/Prices Fork Road to VA 652 and turn right. Follow about 6 miles until you reach the river and VA 625. Turn left and park. Then cross the railroad tracks to get to the Parrot area of the river. This is ideal water for wading and fly-fishermen. If you turn right and travel down VA 625 about a mile you will locate McCoy rapids, also a great area for wading.

While I was a student at Virginia Tech, there were many days when I would anxiously await the end of an afternoon class so that I could jump in my truck and head out Prices Fork Road to the river. The drive is short enough from Blacksburg that you can easily be fishing below the McCoy rapids (Class III) within a half hour of departure. Many students take advantage of this fact in the summer months, so the McCoy rapids are often crowded with sunbathers, "tubers," and fishermen. For that reason, I usually head downstream and across the river to wade. To get there from McCoy, take VA 625 north about 7 miles to VA 730, turn left and cross the Eggleston bridge, then take the first left onto VA 622 that will bring you across the railroad tracks. Go back upstream and fish anywhere you can park and access the river.

Smallmouth are abundant throughout this stretch, although they are rarely big, probably because of the fishing pressure. Still, the water through this stretch of the river is gorgeous and inviting on a summer day. In the afternoon, it is common to see smallmouth literally jumping all around you as you fish. But be careful wading this area. The river can be deceptive; ledges drop off quickly and the small sets of falls that line this part of the river can quickly sweep the most agile wader from his or her feet. Always wear a floatation vest when wading the numerous sets of Class I–II rapids here. The river level is also prone to fluctuation due to the Claytor Dam upstream. Tragically, every few years a student drowns here. I have been told that the Native Americans called the deceptive New "the river of death," and I understand why.

I like to fish this water with ultralight spinning tackle. A day of catching thirty to forty 10- to 14-inch smallmouth on 4-pound test can be a lot of fun. You are also likely to catch a number of good-sized rock bass, or "redeyes" as well. Here, I fish almost exclusively

McCoy Falls, New River, Montgomery County

topwater (Zara Puppies, Pop-R's, and Tiny Torpedoes) or plastic baits (Mister Twister grubs, Yamamoto double-tailed grubs, salted 4-inch worms, and flukes). Many of the locals fish spring lizards and mud puppies, both of which will work if you wish to fish live bait.

This stretch of water can offer some angling surprises. Three interesting stories come to mind: On one occasion, I caught a 16-inch rainbow trout that had apparently washed down from one of the stocked creeks nearby. Another time, while wading a deep hole, Ray Hart hooked a smallie that attracted the attention of a nearby muskie. I'll never forget the expression on his face as he unwittingly struggled against the muskie for that smallmouth until they both saw each other through the crystal-clear water about 10 feet apart. He yelled, and the muskie let go of the ailing smallmouth that was brought in shredded and bleeding. Finally, on yet another occasion, a fishing buddy by the name of Bill Deaver set hook on a fish while using a Yamamoto grub below a rapid in about 2 feet of water only to have the hook straightened out as the fish caught the current and headed downstream.

BIG FISH TIP *Go with soft plastics.*

Giles County

Eggleston (off VA 622) **to Pembroke** (off VA 623)
DISTANCE: 5.5 miles
VIRGINIA ATLAS AND GAZETTEER: 41
DIRECTIONS: (1) *Put-in.* Head west from Blacksburg on U.S. 460, then turn left on VA 730, just before crossing Sinking Creek. Follow

until you cross the Eggleston bridge. Take the first left once across the river, onto VA 622. Take a right once you cross the railroad tracks and meet the river. There is an informal boat launch just upriver. (2) *Take-out.* Go west from Blacksburg on U.S. 460 to the town of Pembroke. Turn left at the sign indicating a VDGIF public boat landing. After a short distance, turn left onto VA 623 and follow to the launch. *Note:* The best route for shuttling from the take-out to the put-in is to backtrack to U.S. 460 and follow the directions to the put-in.

This float starts near the historic landmark known as the Eggleston Palisades. These are the legendary cliffs where Mary Ingels was found after her abduction and escape from the Shawnee Indians in 1755. These breathtaking cliffs are merely a preface to the

New River, Giles County

beautiful river landscape that this float holds. Scenic bluffs curve along the east side of the river throughout much of the float. Again, cabins are few and far between and there is plenty of good fishing through sets of enjoyable Class I rapids.

As the Eggleston Cliffs are passing out of sight you will cross your first set of rapids. I would start fishing bait-casting outfits and spinnerbaits from here on out—chartreuse in the summer, yellow and white in the spring, and darker colors in the fall. Cast them right to the bank and make a slow-rolling retrieve. Another good bait in this area, as throughout the New, is a tube jig. For colors, I like chartreuse or pearl white in the spring and smoke or grape with red flake in the summer.

About halfway through this trip is an excellent stretch of water known as Horse Shoe Bend that can produce some nice small-mouths. A series of shoals create some tricky Class II rapids as you near the last mile or so of the float. This is a favorite trip for many outdoor writers and guides. On a good day, you can expect to land a number of fish in the 2- to 3-pound range.

BIG FISH TIP *Use spinner baits.*

Pembroke (VA 623) **to Ripplemead** (VA 636) **to Bluff City** (under U.S. 460 bridge near Pearisburg)

DISTANCE: 2.5 miles to Ripplemead; 10 miles from Pembroke to Bluff City

VIRGINIA ATLAS AND GAZETTEER: 41–40

DIRECTIONS: (1) *Put-in.* Go west from Blacksburg on U.S. 460 to the town of Pembroke, then turn left at the sign indicating a VDGIF public boat landing. After a short distance, turn left onto VA 623 and follow to the launch. (2a) *Take-out at Ripplemead.* From Blacksburg, travel on U.S. 460 west to the Ripplemead/VA 636 exit. Follow VA 636 until it brings you to the river and back under the U.S. 460 bridge. There you will find informal places to launch. (2b) *Take-out at Bluff City.* Take U.S. 460 west past Pearisburg to the U.S. 460 bridge that crosses over the New River. Exit right before crossing and go back under the bridge. You will find an informal boat launch there.

The first stretch of this two-section float is a short trip of only about 2.5 miles with a rolling Class II rapid near the start. The small islands along this stretch of the river generally hold fish on their downstream ends. This is a good float to make if you are in the Blacksburg area, especially if you need to rent a canoe. New River Canoe Livery is in Pembroke and will provide transportation to and from the put-in and pick-up points of the float.

There is some excellent fishing on the second section of this float and some spectacular scenery. Beware: there are also some formidable Class II rapids to negotiate throughout. I have had good luck in the summer with soft plastics, especially flukes, on this stretch of water. The second section is a long float of over 8 miles that is popular with both canoeists and fishermen alike for its whitewater and proximity to Blacksburg. A good landmark to note is the train trestle a third of the way into the float.

BIG FISH TIP *Try flukes and tube jigs.*

Bluff City (under U.S. 460 bridge near Pearisburg) **to Narrows** (VA 649) **to Glen Lyn** (public boat landing on U.S. 460).

DISTANCE: 4 miles to Narrows; 10 miles from Bluff City to Glen Lyn

VIRGINIA ATLAS AND GAZETTEER: 40

DIRECTIONS: (1) *Put-in.* Take U.S. 460 west past Pearisburg to the U.S. 460 bridge that crosses over the New River. Exit right before crossing and go back under the bridge. You will find an informal boat launch there. (2a) *Take-out at Narrows.* Travel U.S. 460 west to Narrows and turn right at the VA 61 bridge, then cross back over the river to your left. Take a right at VA 649 and look for the public boat landing sign. (2b) *Take-out at Glen Lyn.* Follow U.S. 460 west toward the state line. You will see a sign indicating a public boat

New River at Narrows Falls

landing on your left before crossing the New River and entering into West Virginia.

As a whole, this is a 10-mile float with a little of everything from whitewater to boulders and rock ledges that offer some outstanding fishing. The first section is about 4 miles in length and ends at the public boat landing on river left, just below the Narrows bridge (VA 61). There is an angry Class III rapid on the second part of the float (Narrows Falls) that should be approached with extreme caution and must be scouted first. For the wary, I suggest a portage at the public boat landing mentioned above, which is about a half mile above the falls. If you decide to go on, there is an informal boat launch on river left just below this set of rapids that can be reached from VA 649, and there is a public boat landing a couple of miles further on the right (U.S. 460) above Rich Creek where you can reenter.

The river runs the rest of the way along U.S. 460 to the public campground and boat launch at Glen Lyn, and can be accessed by shore fishermen at numerous other points. There are a few Class I rapids, offering good fishing in their tailwaters, and lots of shallow underwater rocks and ledges that hold fish. Note that the current gets slow in places and can require some paddling. On this stretch of the river I prefer to fish three perennial favorites of fishermen on the New: topwater, buzzbaits, and jig-and-pig. There is also some deep, slow water that is well suited for working a plastic jig or worm.

BIG FISH TIP *One sure bet here is a pumpkinseed 6-inch worm, Texas rigged.*

Glen Lyn (public boat landing on U.S. 460) **to State Line Falls** (or Wylie Falls) **to Bluestone Wildlife Management Area** (WV)– **Shanklins Ferry Landing**

DISTANCE: 4.5 miles to State Line Falls (or Wylie Falls); 6 miles from Glen Lyn to Bluestone Wildlife Management Area (WV)–Shanklins Ferry Landing

VIRGINIA ATLAS AND GAZETTEER: 40

DIRECTIONS: (1) *Put-in at Glen Lyn.* Follow U.S. 460 west toward the state line. You will see a sign indicating a public boat landing on your left before crossing the New River and entering into West Virginia. (2a) *Take-out at State Line Falls (or Wylie Falls).* Drive across the New River on U.S. 460 and turn right onto VA 648; follow this road into West Virginia (Mercer County) where it becomes Bluff Rd. Stay on the hardtop. Follow it approximately 4 miles up a mountainside until it ends and turn right. This road will soon turn into gravel and will lead to the State Line Falls. There is a good informal take-out just above the falls. (2b) *Take-out at Bluestone Wildlife Management Area (WV)–Shanklins Ferry Landing.* Take U.S. 460 to Rich Creek and turn onto U.S. 219 north. Follow about 2 miles to Peterstown, then turn left onto WV 12. Go 1 mile to WV 24 and turn left. Take this road approximately 5 miles to Shanklins Ferry Road and turn left. This will take you directly into the Bluestone Wildlife Management Area and the Shanklins Ferry Camping Area and Landing. *Note:* An alternative put-in can be found by crossing the New River on U.S. 460 at Glen Lyn and turning right onto VA 648, then taking the dirt road to the right off of VA 648 at the Mercer County line. This road will take you all the way to the State Line Falls and eventually out to Bluff Road. There are numerous informal put-ins along this road; however, this is rugged "bottom," owned and (poorly) maintained by the Army Corps of Engineers, that requires a four-wheel drive to traverse.

This float is simply fantastic and should require a full day of fishing. There are numerous ledges and two major sets of rapids/falls to fish through. There are also some long, deep stretches of river that hold lunker smallmouth. There is some notable white-water just down from the U.S. 460 bridge (and put-in) that is difficult to fish; however, the eddies in this area hold some nice smallmouth for those who can manage to get a cast in. The first set of falls (Class III–IV) occurs about 2 miles into the float and is a favorite place for local fishermen to wade. These must be negotiated through the middle when the river is up, or portaged on the left when low. Do not attempt to run these without scouting first. You will find some excellent fishing between here and the state line. I suggest taking out above the second set of falls at the state line; there is a nice informal launch on river left. You may also choose to continue the float into West Virginia and take out at Bluestone Wildlife Management Area. In this case, stay to the far right of the canal wall. (Also, you'll need a West Virginia fishing license.) This is a fairly large and remote managed game and fish area, with plenti-ful primitive camping ($8 per night—honor system). There are three separate boat launching areas, and the float can be extended by taking out at either Indian Creek or Bertha landings. Many of the locals take pride in the tremendous catfishing that is found in this part of the New River, while large Kentucky spotted bass are also plentiful.

I last made this trip with Mike Keith on a warm day in April on which we witnessed bass feeding heavily on a late-afternoon mayfly hatch. We had success using spinnerbaits with fire-tail trailers, crayfish-colored Bagley's crankbaits, and 4-inch worms.

BIG FISH TIP *Camp at Bluestone Wildlife Management Area and use live bait for catfish at night.*

Appendix: Information and Resources

General Inquiries, Licenses, etc.

Virginia Department of Game and Inland Fisheries
4010 West Broad St.
Richmond, VA 23230
(804) 367-1000
http://www.dgif.state.va.us/

VDGIF Blacksburg Office
Draper Aden Building
2206 S. Main St./Suite C
Blacksburg, VA 24060
(540) 951-7923

Camping

Blacksburg Ranger District—Jefferson National Forest
110 South Park Dr.
Blacksburg, VA 24060
(540) 552-4641

Bluestone Wildlife Management Area
HC-65, Box 91
Indian Mills, WV 24935
(304) 466-3398

Claytor Lake State Park
4400 State Park Rd.
Dublin, VA 24084
(540) 674-5492 or (800) 933-7275

New River Trail State Park
176 Orphanage Drive
Foster Falls, VA 24360
(540) 699-6778

Virginia State Parks Division
203 Governor St., Suite 306
Richmond, VA 23219
(804) 786-1712

Guides and Outfitters

Mike Smith, Greasy Creek Outfitters
P.O. Box 211
Willis, VA 24380
(540) 789-7811
www.greasycreekoutfitters.com

Tangent Outfitters
4747 State Park Rd.
Dublin, VA 24084
(540) 674-5202
www.newrivertrail.com

Liveries

Blue Cat on the New
2800 Wysor Hwy.
Draper, VA 24324
(276) 766-3729

New River Adventures
Foster Falls State Park
(540) 699-1034
www.newriveradventures.com

New River Canoe Livery
U.S. 460, Pembroke, VA
(540) 626-7189

Riverside Outfitters
12 Scenic Rd.
Fries, VA 24330
www.riversideoutfitters.com

Lodging and Food

Chateau Morrisette
Box 766
Meadows of Dan, VA
(540)593-2865

Doe Run Lodge
M.P. 189 Blue Ridge Parkway
Fancy Gap, VA 24328
(800) 325-6189

Goose Creek Mountain Resort
Floyd, VA
(540) 651-3800

Harmony Farm Bed and Breakfast
3510 Black Ridge Rd., SW
Floyd, VA 24091
www.harmony-farm.com

Mountain Lake Resort
115 Hotel Circle
Mountain Lake, VA 24136
(540) 626-7121

Pine Tavern
585 Floyd Hwy. North
Floyd, VA 24091
(540) 745-4428

Riverbend Farm Bed and Breakfast
225 Zells Mill Rd.
Newport, VA 24128
(888)-835-9374

River's Edge
6208 Little Camp Rd.
Riner, VA 24149
(540) 381-4147

Woodberry Inn and Restaurant
182 Woodberry Rd. Southwest
Meadows of Dan, VA
(540) 593-2567

Maps

Virginia Atlas and Gazeteer, 4th edition (Yarmouth, Maine: DeLorme, 2000). ISBN 0-8993-3326-5. (Widely available at bookstores and online sources, or see www.delorme.com for information)

Claytor Lake
Cartex Co.
Rt. 3, Box 164-C
Pulaski, VA 24301

New River
River Maps LTD
P.O. Box 357
Radford, VA 24141

Marinas (Claytor Lake)

Conrad Bros. Marine
Route 100
Pulaski, VA 24301
(540) 980-1575

K&K Marine
Exit 101, I-81
Dublin, VA
(540) 674-4621

Lakeside Marine Supply
Exit 101, I-81
Dublin, VA
(540) 674-0908

Rock House Marina
RFD 2
Pulaski, VA
(540) 980-1488

Rod and Reel Repair

Thompson Rod and Reel Repair
1771 Radford Road (Rt. 11)
P.O. Box 186
Christiansburg, VA 24073
(540) 382-9477

Tackle Shops in the New River Valley

Big Z Bass Pro Dealer
Radford Shopping Plaza
(540) 639-1651

Blacksburg Feed and Seed
1212 N. Main St.
Blacksburg, VA
(540) 552-1631

The Sportsman's
Radford Dam on Little River Rd.
Radford, VA
(540) 639-0599

Orvis
19 Campbell Ave.
Roanoke, VA
(540) 345-3635

Index

Page references to photographs are in boldface